TEACHING PHONICS
AND OTHER
WORD ATTACK SKILLS

TEACHING PHONICS
AND OTHER
WORD ATTACK SKILLS

By

THOMAS G. GUNNING, Ed.D.

Reading Department
Southern Connecticut State University

CHARLES C THOMAS • PUBLISHER
Springfield • Illinois • U.S.A.

Published and Distributed Throughout the World by

CHARLES C THOMAS • PUBLISHER

2600 South First Street

Springfield, Illinois 62794-9265

© *1988 by* CHARLES C THOMAS • PUBLISHER

ISBN 0-398-05486-X

Library of Congress Catalog Card Number: 88-9421

With THOMAS BOOKS *careful attention is given to all details of manufacturing and
design. It is the Publisher's desire to present books that are satisfactory as to their physical
qualities and artistic possibilities and appropriate for their particular use.* THOMAS
BOOKS *will be true to those laws of quality that assure a good name and good will.*

Printed in the United States of America
Q-R-3

Library of Congress Cataloging in Publication Data

Gunning, Thomas G.
    Teaching phonics and other word attack skills / by Thomas G.
Gunning.
        p.   cm.
    Bibliography: p.
    Includes index.
    ISBN 0-398-05486-X
    1. Reading (Elementary)--Phonetic method. I. Title.
LB1573.3G86   1988
372.4'145--dc19   88-9421
                                                                      CIP

To Joy, Timothy, and Faith

PREFACE

TEACHING Phonics and Other Word Attack Skills is designed to be a practical tool for the classroom teacher and the reading specialist, the novice and the seasoned professional. Although all major word attack skills have been included in the text, the most extensive coverage has been given to the teaching of phonics, since this is the most fundamental and the most complex of the word attack skills.

Chapter I explains the three main approaches to the teaching of phonics, their advantages and disadvantages, and some basic principles for teaching phonics, regardless of approach used. Chapter II explains the content of phonics, the sounds of the language and their spellings. Chapters III, IV, V, VI, and VII demonstrate how various word attack elements might be taught.

Chapters VIII, IX, and X explore special problems involved in the teaching of word attack skills. Chapter VIII contains suggestions for helping disabled readers. Chapter IX explores techniques for handling diverse dialects. Chapter X makes suggestions for adapting word attack instruction for youngsters whose native tongue is not English.

Chapter XI describes resources for teaching word attack skills. Listed are workbooks, kits, computer software, children's books, games, and other manipulatives. Chapter XII discusses techniques for assessing word attack skills and lists a number of tests. Also included is an informal word attack test, which the reader is free to use.

Emphasis throughout the text is on instruction. Although materials are listed, it has been the author's experience that careful teaching is what makes the difference. Much of the text is devoted to providing sample lessons and ideas for practice. Lists of words accompany each word attack skill covered in the text so the teacher will have a ready supply of examples to use for presenting a skill or creating exercises to reinforce the skill.

Pronunciations listed in the text are based on those contained in *Webster's Ninth New Collegiate Dictionary* (Mish, 1983). In those instances where two or three pronunciations were listed for a particular word, the first was chosen. As a practical matter it wasn't feasible to include all legitimate pronunciations. Readers will need to adapt the text to fit their dialects and those of their students.

CONTENTS

TEACHING PHONICS
AND OTHER
WORD ATTACK SKILLS

CHAPTER I

THE TEACHING OF PHONICS:
APPROACHES AND PRINCIPLES

THE Great Debate is over. For many years there was a heated controversy over whether it was best to teach students to read by using a sight approach or by using phonics. Today there is general agreement that phonics is an essential part of reading instruction. In *What Works* (U.S. Department of Education, 1986), a compilation of basic educational practices that are well supported by research, the authors conclude that:

> Children get a better start in reading if they are taught phonics. Learning phonics helps them to understand the relationship between letters and sounds and "to break the code" that links the words they hear with the words they see in print. (p. 21)

This finding echoes conclusions drawn by Chall (1967, 1983), Dykstra (1974), and Anderson (1985). There is less agreement on how to teach phonics. Aukerman (1984) described 165 approaches to beginning reading, most of which employ a decoding strand. These and other approaches fall into one of three main methods for teaching phonics or decoding skills: the analytic, the synthetic, and the linguistic spelling pattern, which, technically, is not a phonics system.

THE ANALYTIC APPROACH

Judging by sales of basal readers, the most popular approach by far is the analytic. Approximately 85 percent of the nation's school children use a basal that employs an analytic approach. The analytic approach teaches phonics through whole words. The sounds of letters are never isolated. A teacher talks about the sound heard at the beginning of **man,**

3

moon, and monkey but never says /m/. Technically, this is an accurate way to present consonant sounds. As linguist Leonard Bloomfield (1942) noted, isolating the sounds of consonants distorts them.

The major advantage of the analytic approach is that it does not distort sounds. Since it always deals with sounds in whole words, it also tends to be more meaningful. On the other hand, the analytic approach uses roundabout terminology—"the sound heard at the beginning of man, moon, and monkey"—and requires the learner to abstract the sound from the word. The student must abstract the sound of /m/ from the series of sounds heard in man, moon, or monkey. This is not an easy task and is a major stumbling block for some youngsters.

THE SYNTHETIC APPROACH

The synthetic approach isolates consonant as well as vowel sounds. The teacher might say something like: "The letter m stands for /m/. Say /m/." In decoding the word bat, students would isolate each sound and then blend them together (buh-ah-tuh—bat).

The synthetic approach is more immediate. The student does not have to abstract the sound from a word. The language of instruction is also more direct. The teacher talks about /m/ rather than the sound heard at the beginning of man, moon, and monkey.

Unfortunately, in the synthetic approach, the sounds are distorted, and blending, which is required by a synthetic approach, can be a difficult obstacle to surmount. Students might concentrate on isolated sounds and not realize that they are supposed to be pronouncing words. One young student when asked by her parents what she had done at school that day replied: "puh-ih-tuh." The child had learned the sounding out part of the lesson well but had failed to blend the sounds into a meaningful word: pit. Part of the child's problem may have been that the word pit was not part of her listening vocabulary. The word was chosen for inclusion in the program because it was easy to decode. A major shortcoming of synthetic programs as presently constructed is that they tend to stress sounding out to the detriment of meaning.

LINGUISTIC SPELLING PATTERNS

A third major approach to the teaching of decoding skills does not involve phonics. Students learn decoding skills through a process of contrast and induction. In a linguistic spelling pattern approach, a series of words is placed on the board. For instance, the words **cat, bat, sat, fat** would be written one underneath the other on the chalkboard. The teacher reads the words or the students read the words if they can. Each word is then spelled. And each word is contrasted with the word before it. After studying hundreds of patterns, students are expected to learn automatically the sound represented by various letters and letter combinations.

Technically, there are no flaws in this approach. Sounds are neither distorted nor divorced from real words. Consonants and vowels are learned together in word context. No roundabout language is used. The method is economical and step-by-step. Students learn a group of similar elements at the same time. Usually, these elements or patterns are practiced immediately in story selections.

Unfortunately, in their attempt to control patterns, creators of linguistic materials have found themselves forced to restrict the words they use. This has sometimes led to selections that tend to be artificial. This becomes less of a problem as more patterns are introduced. As the authors find themselves with a larger store of words, language becomes more natural, and selections become more interesting.

THE BEST APPROACH

Which approach is best? Research is so limited that it is impossible to say which approach is most effective. Both the U.S. Department of Education (1986) and the Commission on Reading as reported in Anderson (1985), although favoring synthetic phonics, recommend incorporating features of both analytic and synthetic techniques.

Children tend to be pragmatic about the techniques they use to decode difficult words. A group of 41 second graders, some of whom had been taught an analytic phonics approach and some of whom had been taught synthetic phonics, used a variety of approaches to decode difficult words (Gunning, 1986). Many pronounced the initial consonant in isolation but said the rest of the words as a whole. For example, in reading the word **chip,** several students said "ch-ip." Others started with pronounceable elements that were longer than a single sound but shorter than a word. When reading the word **with,** for instance, students pronounced it as "wi-with." When reading **spot,** students read "ot-spot." What the majority of sudents seemed to be doing was seeking units that are easily pronounced and which would help them pronounce the whole word. In a sense, they seemed to be using elements of the analytic, synthetic, and word pattern approach. Interestingly, although half the students had been taught with a strong synthetic phonics approach, few attempted to decode words sound by sound.

Teachers might follow the lead of these second graders and develop a pragmatic approach to the teaching of phonics. There may be some students who do better with a synthetic approach than they do with an analytic one and vice versa. Or perhaps a linguistic spelling pattern approach might work best. If students are having difficulty grasping consonants taught analytically, the teacher might try presenting them in isolation. This works especially well with the consonants (/s/, /m/, /f/, and similarly formed sounds) because distortion tends to be minimal when these sounds are pronounced in isolation. Conversely, students struggling with a synthetic phonics or linguistic approach might do better with one that emphasizes context or meaning. In the absence of definitive research indicating the superiority of one approach to teaching phonics, teachers should weigh the strengths and weaknesses of each and use whatever works best in a particular situation. The most effective approach may be an amalgam of the best features of the analytic, the synthetic, and the linguistic techniques.

VARIATIONS WITHIN APPROACHES

Most of America's students learn to read through an analytic approach. Major analytic programs are listed in Table I. Although they are all analytic, these programs vary in terms of intensity of phonics. The most significant differences can be seen in the way vowels are handled. Some of the programs—*Houghton, Mifflin,* and *Scott, Foresman,* for example—opt for a more gradual introduction of vowels. On the other hand, *Heath* and *Ginn* use patterns to introduce vowels fairly early and *Scribner's,* with its analytic/pattern focus, features a high intensity approach to phonics.

Major synthetic approaches are listed in Table II. There is probably more variance among synthetic programs than there is among analytic programs. For example, *Keys to Reading* is often used with brighter-than-average youngsters since this program seems to move at a fairly rapid pace. *Reading Mastery* (formerly *Distar*), on the other hand, moves at a more deliberate pace and is often used with disadvantaged youngsters. There are also differences in sequence among synthetic programs. Most series start with short vowels. However, *Open Court, Keys to Reading,* and *Keytext* introduce long vowels before short vowels.

TABLE I
Analytic Reading Programs

American Readers (Heath)
Bookmark Reading Program (Harcourt Brace Jovanovich)
Focus (Scott, Foresman)
Ginn Readers (Ginn)
Harper & Row Reading Program (Harper & Row)
Holt Basic Reading (Holt, Rinehart, & Winston)
Houghton Mifflin Reading (Houghton Mifflin)
New Directions in Reading (Houghton Mifflin)[1]
Reading Express (Macmillan)
Riverside Reading Series (Riverside)
Scribner Reading Series (Scribner)
Scott, Foresman Reading (Scott, Foresman)
Series R (Macmillan)

TABLE II
Synthetic Reading Programs

Addison-Wesley Reading Program (Addison-Wesley)
Keytext (McGraw-Hill)
Keys to Reading (McGraw-Hill)
Mott (Allied Educational Council)[1]
Open Court Reading Program (Open Court)
PALS (IBM)[1,2]
Programmed Reading (McGraw-Hill)
Reading Mastery (SRA)
Reading 2000 (Random House)[1]
Steck-Vaughn Adult Reading (Steck Vaughn)[1]
Writing to Read (IBM)[2]

TABLE III
Linguistic Patterns

Merrill Linguistic Readers (Merrill)
Basic Reading Series (SRA)

BASIC PRINCIPLES OF TEACHING PHONICS

Regardless of approach used, there are certain basic principles of teaching phonics. These include:

• Phonics should be taught as a tool for decoding words. Phonics is not a body of knowledge worth knowing for its own sake. Exercises that involve marking vowels long or short or finding schwa are probably useless. A better activity would be reading selections that contain long or short vowels or schwas.

• Once students have some facility decoding words, they no longer need instruction in this skill. The Commission on Reading (Anderson, 1985) recommends that phonics instruction be completed by the end of the second grade, except where there is a special need. This is, of course, a rough rule of thumb. There are some advanced elements that might not be introduced until third grade or later — ti = /sh/, for example.

• Phonics skills should be directly and immediately applied. The only reason for teaching the **oa** spelling of long **o** as in **boat** or any other correspondence is that the element will be needed to read an upcoming selection. The best time to teach the **oa** spelling of /ō/ would be just before students read a story such as "The Three Billy Goats Gruff" or an article about boats.

• Emphasis should be placed upon application rather than the learning of generalizations. Except for final **e,** students don't make very effective use of generalizations (Gunning, 1986). Although it is useful to formulate some of the high frequency generalizations, it is better to read selections that contain words that follow the generalization than it is to spend an excessive amount of time memorizing generalizations, especially those that cover a limited number of words or which have many exceptions.

• Phonics should be integrated with other word attack skills, especially context. In many situations, it is almost impossible to use phonics properly without also using context. For example, in the sentence, "The pipe was made of lead," it would be impossible to give an accurate pronunciation of the word **lead** without using context.

• Getting meaning must be the underlying objective of phonics instruction. Students sometimes get so involved decoding that they conclude that reading is a matter of saying sounds. Often they produce nonsense words or words that don't fit the context. For example, a number of second graders read "kitty" for "city" in the following sentence from a story in which young people were on their way to catch a train: "Mike drove the girls to the city" (Gunning, 1986). While it is true that the letter **c** most frequently represents /k/, context should have alerted students to the fact that **city** makes sense in the sentence but **kitty** doesn't. These youngsters failed to integrate phonics with context.

• Students need to be taught to be flexible in their use of phonics. Many phonics elements may represent more than one sound. The letters **ow,** for example, most frequently represent /ō/ as in **snow** but may also represent /ow/ as in **now.** If the students give this vowel combination the long **o** pronunciation and this does not produce a real word and one that makes sense in context, they should attempt the /ow/ pronunciation.

Footnotes

1. Designed for older readers
2. Computer assisted programs

CHAPTER II

THE CONTENT OF PHONICS

ALTHOUGH phonics is an integral, nearly universal part of reading instruction, it is also a confusing subject. You may have puzzled over one or more of the following questions: What vowel and consonant generalizations should be taught? What is a digraph? What is a glide? A dipthong? How many vowels are there? Is **w** a vowel?

Part of the confusion in phonics arises from the fact that it is a complex area that is often oversimplified and/or poorly defined. Phonics is the study of the relationship between speech sounds and their spellings. Phonics can be very confusing if no distinction is made between sounds and spellings. A few years ago, a colleague, obviously irritated, asked me when **w** became a vowel. The point of confusion was in the word **vowel.** The word **vowel** is commonly used to refer to a speech sound and the spelling of a sound. There is no vowel sound known as the **w** vowel. However, the letter **w** can be used along with another letter to spell vowel sounds: /ow/ in **now,** /aw/ in **paw,** or /ō/ in **snow.**

In the same vein, many people believe that there are five or six vowels: **a, e, i, o, u** and sometimes **y.** Actually, there are approximately 16 vowel sounds. However, these sounds are frequently represented by the letters, **a, e, i, o, u,** and **y.**

To avoid confusion, this text when using the words **vowel** or **consonant** will be referring to sounds, except when **vowel** or **consonant** is followed by the word **letter.** In addition, sounds will be placed between slash marks; letters representing sounds will be bold. The expression **ph**=/f/, for example, means that the letters **ph** represent the sound heard at the beginning of **photo.**

CONSONANTS

In English, there are two major kinds of sounds: consonants and vowels. Consonants are the backbone of most phonics programs. Because

11

consonant letters have more predictability than vowel letters, they are introduced first in most reading programs. Research (Marchbanks and Levin, 1965) also indicates that the first and last letters of a word, which are frequently consonant letters, are the most helpful in decoding unknown words.

Technically, consonants are speech sounds that are formed by obstructing the stream of breath. There are 25 consonant sounds. Consonant letters are said to be "regular." That is a consonant letter usually represents a single sound. The letter **b,** for instance, regularly stands for the sound heard at the beginning and end of **Bob.** However, *Webster's Ninth New Collegiate Dictionary* (Mish, 1983) provides more than 175 different ways to spell consonant sounds. The sound /t/, for example, is listed as being spelled in the following ways: **tea, debt, ctenoid, ptomaine, thyme, button, yacht, night, phthisic** (p. 39).

Listed below is a chart of the 25 consonants with some common and some less frequent spellings. Note that the sound listed as /hw/ is not present in all dialects. It is the sound produced by people pronouncing **whale** and **when** as /hwal/ and /hwen/.

TABLE IV
Consonant Spellings

/b/	buy, robber	/s/	soap, horse, center
/d/	day, ladder, loved	/t/	tie, letter, walked
/f/	fun, puff, nephew, laugh	/v/	vine, have
/g/	go, guest, egg, ghost, exit	/w/	wet, wheel, queen, one
/h/	how, who	/y/	yellow, onion
/hw/	when, where	/z/	zero, dozen, puzzle, cousin,
/j/	juice, hedge, soldier, magic,		xylophone, nose, freeze
	education	/ch/	church, match, question, nature
/k/	key, come, tick, square,	/sh/	ship, sugar, machine, nation,
	Christmas, account		ocean, issue
/l/	lap, till	/th/	think
/m/	me, autumn, climb	/th/	them
/n/	not, running, knife	/zh/	measure, beige, division
/p/	pie, supper	/ng/	sing, sink
/r/	rip, marry		

DIGRAPHS

Some consonant sounds are spelled with single letters. Others are represented by a combination of letters. For example, in the words **boy** and **tea,** the initial sounds are represented by the single letters **b** and **t.** In the words **chop** and **ship,** however, the initial sounds are represented by two letters each. Pairs of letters that represent single sounds are known as digraphs. Technically, the double letters in **bell** and **butter** are also digraphs, since in both words a pair of letters is used to represent a single sound. The major consonant digraphs are:

/ch/ — church	/th/ — thick
/ŋ/ — thing	/th/ — this
/sh/ — shirt	/wh/ — whip

Because digraphs use two letters to spell a single sound, there is a temptation to think of digraphs as having two sounds. However, this is not so. Both **sugar** and **sheet** begin with the same single sound, although the sound is spelled with an **s** and an **sh.**

PROBLEM CONSONANT LETTERS

Consonant sounds have a more predictable spelling than vowel sounds. However, there are several consonant letters that pose particular problems. These include **c, g, qu, s,** and **x.** As noted in Table V, **c, g,** and final **s** regularly represent two sounds. The letter **x** is a reverse digraph. It regularly represents /ks/ as in **box** and /gz/ as in **exist** but less frequently spells /z/ as in **xylophone.** The letters **qu** are superfluous since they regularly represent /kw/, a sound that could just as well be signified by **kw.**

TABLE V

Problem Consonants

c = /k/	cake, cut		−s = /z/	toys, is
c = /s/	city, cedar		qu = /kw/	queen, quick
g = /g/	gum, got		x = /ks/	box, mix
g = /j/	gym, ginger		x = /gz/	exist, examine
−s = /s/	plus, mess		x = /z/	xylophone

CLUSTERS

Although there are 25 consonant sounds, many of these sounds are combined into clusters of two or three beginning or ending sounds. The word, **bring,** for example, begins with the cluster **br** (/b/ + /r/); the word **string** starts with three sounds /s/ + /t/ + /r/. Clusters are also commonly called blends. Most clusters involve /s/, /l/, or /r/. The most common initial clusters are listed in Table VI.

TABLE VI
Initial Clusters

---

l — bl, cl, fl, gl, pl, sl
r — br, cr, dr, fr, gr, pr
s — sc, sch, scr, sl, sm, sn, sp, st, sw
other — tw, qu

Note that the letters **sc** would be a digraph in a word like **scientist** because they would represent the single sound /s/. In **scare, sc** would be a cluster because the letters would stand for /sk/.

Most clusters, such as **sm** and **gr,** occur only at the beginning of words. A few, such as **st (stop, best)** and **sk (skip, task),** may occur in both initial and final positions. Some other clusters, such as **-nt (bent)** and **-nd (lend),** occur only in final position. Common ending clusters are contained in Table VII.

TABLE VII
Ending Clusters

---

l — lm, lp, lt
n — nce, nch, nd, ng, nge, nk, nt
s — sk[1], st[1]
other — ct, mp

VOWELS

Vowels are speech sounds that are produced with a relatively unobstructed stream of air. Vowels are also the center of a word or syllable. Vowels are less predictable in their spellings than consonants are. There are approximately 16 vowels in English. However, these 16 vowels can be spelled in more than 200 ways. For instance, the sound /ō/ can be spelled **no, note, boat, toe, sew, show, though, bureau, quahog,** and **pharoah.** On the other side of the coin, the letter **o** can represent the vowel sounds heard in **note, not, do, ton, woman,** and **women.** The list would be even longer if digraphs containing an **o** were included.

All of this suggests that English has a hopelessly irregular spelling system. This is not true. While each vowel sound can be spelled in a variety of ways, many of these varied spellings are rare. Some only occur once. Generally, each vowel has one or two spellings that account for 90 percent or more of its occurrences. Listed in Table VIII are the English vowels and some of their common spellings.

TABLE VIII
Vowel Spellings

Short Vowels		Long Vowels	
/a/	hat, ladder	/ā/	gate, paper, hay, rain
/e/	bell, insect, bread	/ē/	he, these, even, bee, bean, city
/i/	fish, hitter, gym	/ī/	mine, light, bicycle, why
/o/	lock, rocket, father	/ō/	no, note, gold, boat, snow, bureau
/u/	bus, butter, glove, young	/ū/	mule, few
Other Vowels		**R-Vowels**	
/aw/	hawk, fault, ball, salt	/er/	bird, nurse, word, earth
/oi/	boy, soil	/ar/	car, heart
/ŏŏ/	foot, pull, could	/air/	canary, chair, bear, square
/ōō/	moon, suit, two, new	/ear/	beard, deer, hero
/ow/	owl, out	/or/	order, horse
/ə/	above, secretary, animal, collect, upon		

From a linguist's point of view there are only 16 vowels. However, this book lists 21 vowels. The **r**-vowels listed in Table VIII are not distinct vowels. However, these elements are listed as separate vowels because they are commonly treated as such by reading teachers.

Although not used by linguists, the terms "long" and "short" vowels have also been retained because these are familiar to teachers. At one time, the pronunciation of some vowels was of greater duration than that of other vowels, so the terms "long" and "short" had a functional meaning. Today linguists often use the word **glide** to describe long vowels because the articulatory mechanisms literally glide from one to the other as a long vowel is pronounced.

Footnote

1. Occur in both initial and final position.

CHAPTER III

THE TEACHING OF CONSONANTS

TEACHING CONSONANT RELATIONSHIPS

CONSONANTS can be taught in three main ways: through presentation within the context of a word, by isolating the consonant, or through contrasting patterns. The most popular approach is presentation in context. Known as the analytic approach, this method of presenting consonants is advocated by most of the major basals.

Although details vary from series to series, the analytic approach generally consists of presenting consonants in five steps: auditory discrimination, auditory perception, linking of letter-sound elements within the context of a word, practice, and application. Here is how the correspondence **p** = /p/ might be introduced.

Auditory Discrimination

Auditory discrimination means that students are able to detect slight differences in the sounds of spoken words. If students can't hear the difference between **pen** and **den,** they will be unable to associate the letter **p** with the sound /p/ or the letter **d** with /d/ with any degree of consistency. Because of poor auditory discrimination, the child might actually associate **p** with /d/.

To develop auditory discrimination, present the following activities, which force students to distinguish between similar sounding words.

Activity 1: Hold up the following real objects and ask:

(Holding up a can) Is this a can or a pan?
(Holding up a pin) Is this a pin or a tin?
(Holding up a pen) Is this a ten or a pen?
(Holding up a cup) Is this a cup or a pup?

17

(Holding up a bowl) Is this a pole or a bowl?
(Holding up a pickle) Is this a tickle or a pickle?
(Holding up illustration of dog or cat) Is this a bet or a pet?
(Holding up a peach) Is this a beach or a peach?
(Holding up illustration of cat) Is this a cat or a pat?
(Holding up illustration of bike) Is this a bike or a pike?

Activity 2: Present the following word pairs to students. Have them raise one hand if the words are different and two if they are the same.

List 1		List 2	
pan	pan	pen	Ben
pen	ten	pin	pin
pot	not	pat	bat
pet	pet	pot	dot
pat	pat	pie	pie
paste	waste	pan	Dan
five	five	peach	peach
pole	pole	pig	big
paint	paint	paste	taste
pay	ray	peg	beg

Auditory Perception

Auditory perception means that a student is able to perceive a certain speech sound. In the analytic approach, it involves abstracting that sound from a word.

Activity 1: Hold up a series of objects or illustrations of objects. Have students name each object. Then repeat the name of each object and ask students to tell what is the same about the sound of each object. For example, hold up a pen, pan, peach, pot, pencil. Ask: how are the sounds of **pen, pan, peach, pot,** and **pencil** alike? What is the same about **pen, pan, peach, pot,** and **pencil**? Discuss with students the fact that **pen, pan, peach, pot,** and **pencil** begin with the same sound.

Activity 2: Have students stand up whose first names begin like **pen** (Paul, Patricia). Have students stand up whose last names begin like **pen**.

Activity 3: Play animal riddles. Have students guess the name of animals whose names begin like **pen**. Some sample riddles include:

I live on a farm.
I have little legs but a big body.

My nose is flat.
And I say, "Oink! Oink!" (pig)

I like to eat grass and hay.
I like to run in fields.
I can carry people on my back.
I am bigger than a dog.
But I am smaller than a horse. (pony)

I am a bird.
But my wings are small
And I can not fly.
I live where it is very cold. (penguin)

Activity 4: Play I spy. Say, "I spy something in this room that begins like **pen.**" Have students identify piano, paste, pole, pipe, pencil, pot, paint, or other objects in the room that begin like **pen.** Give added clues as needed.

Linking Letter and Sound

Once students' auditory discrimination and perception of /p/ are adequate, say the names of several objects beginning with /p/ and write their names on the chalkboard: **pen, pan, peach, pot, pencil.** Say the words once more and point to each word as you say it. Remind students that each word begins with the same sound. Ask them what is the same about the way the words look. Lead students to see that each word begins with the letter **p.** Tell students that the letter **p** makes the sound heard at the beginning of **pen, pan, peach, pot,** and **pencil.**

Put the names of students whose names begin with **p** on the chalkboard. Say each student's name as you write it on the board. Explain that people's names begin with capital letters. Point to students' names and the names of the five objects. Tell students that both capital and lowercase **p** stand for the sound heard at the beginning of **pen.**

Practice

• Have students complete workbook pages that contain exercises on the **p**=/p/ correspondence or create practice exercises and games of your own.

• Label objects in your room that begin with **p.** Encourage students to read the labels. After a few days, take the labels away from the objects and see if students can read the labels.

• Display food product containers that have a **p** on their labels. Hold up a can of pumpkin. Ask students to tell which letter stands for the sound heard at the beginning of **pumpkin.** Do the same with sweet peas, whole pears, peanut butter, popcorn, pineapple slices, and potato chips.

• Bring in opaque salt and pepper shakers that are marked with **S** and **P.** Ask students to tell how they can tell which one contains salt and which one contains pepper.

• Read parts of *Mr. Popper's Penguins* or other books in which **p** is prominent to students. Point out or write on the chalkboard some of the main words whose names begin with **p.**

• As a kinesthetic reinforcement, have students practice writing upper and lowercase **p.**

• See p. 28 for additional suggestions.

Application

• Have students read sample stories that contain **p.**

• Have students compose experience stories in which the letter **p** appears. They might write about their pets, the puppy next door, or the polar bear at the zoo.

• Have students practice using the letter **p** and context to decode words. When students meet a word that begins with **p**, encourage them to use the sound of the letter and the meaning of the sentence to figure out what the word is. Also provide practice in this skill by having students tell what words might be used to fill in the sentences below. Remind students that the word they supply must make sense in the sentence and must begin with the sound heard at the beginning of **pen.** If necessary, read the sentences for the students but have them supply possible missing words.

1. I have a cat for a p_____.
2. The man will p_____ my home blue.
3. The ham is in the p_____.
4. Write your name on the p_____.
5. Can you play the p_____?

TEACHING CONSONANTS WITH A SYNTHETIC APPROACH

Consonants are introduced in much the same way in a synthetic approach as they are in an analytic one. The five teaching steps are basically the same. The main difference is that consonants are isolated in synthetic approaches. Instead of referring to /p/ as the sound heard at the beginning of **pen,** the teacher says /p/. Since consonants can't be said without a vowel sound, the teacher says /puh/, which is a distortion of the sound. Here is how the correspondence **p** = /p/ is introduced in the readiness level of the *Economy Reading Series* (Matteoni and others, 1986), a widely-used synthetic approach.

Auditory Discrimination/Perception

The teacher shows a picture of a peach. The children identify the peach and are asked if they hear the sound /p/ at the beginning of **peach.** They are then shown a picture of a top and are asked if they hear /p/ at the end of **top.**

Illustrations of peas, picture, pie, and pipe are shown and discussed. Students are asked to raise their hands if they hear /p/ at the beginning or end of each word.

Linking Letter and Sound

The teacher shows cards that contain upper and lowercase **p.** The teacher explains that **p** is a consonant letter and it stands for the sound heard at the beginning of **peach** and end of **top.**

The word **peach** is written on the chalkboard and the illustration of **peach** is shown. The teacher points to the word **peach** and asks if students heard /p/ at the beginning or end of **peach.** The teacher then explains that the word on the board is **peach** and asks if students see the consonant letter **p** in **peach** and if they hear the /p/ in **peach.** The teacher then asks what letter stands for /p/ in **peach, top, peas, picture, pie,** and **pipe.**

Practice

Later students listen to a story that contains words beginning with **p** and complete a workbook exercise in which they identify pictures whose names begin with /p/. They also identify the letter **p** in words. The **p** = /p/ correspondence is reviewed in two additional lessons.

Application

The correspondence **p** = /p/ is reviewed on the first preprimer level and is applied in a story that contains several words beginning with **p.**

LINGUISTIC PATTERN APPROACH

Consonants are not taught directly in a linguistic approach. Students learn patterns that contain rhyming words (**pat, cat, sat; pan, fan, van**). As they learn patterns, they pay particular attention to the way the pattern words are spelled and how the spelling of one pattern word differs from another. Through experience with many patterns, it is expected they would learn necessary decoding skills, including initial consonant letter-sound relationships.

SEQUENCE OF TEACHING CONSONANTS

In what order should consonants be taught? Obviously, consonant sounds spelled with single letters are taught before single consonants represented by digraphs. However, other than that, the order in which the elements are introduced varies from program to program. One factor that should be considered is frequency of occurrence. Listed in Table IX are consonants grouped according to frequency of appearance.

TABLE IX

Order of Occurrence of Major Consonant Correspondences

r = /r/	**b** = /b/	**ng** = /ŋ/
t = /t/	**c** = /k/	**k** = /k/
n = /n/	**f** = /f/	**ch** = /ch/
s = /s/	**sh** = /sh/	**c** = /s/
l = /l/	**v** = /v/	**g** = /j/
d = /d/	**g** = /g/	**y** = /y/
m = /m/	**j** = /j/	**z** = /z/
p = /p/	**h** = /h/	
	w = /w/	

Another factor that should be considered when presenting consonants is ease of discrimination. Based on manner of production, there are two types of consonant sounds: stops and continuants. Stops are articulated by restricting or stopping the flow of air. The word **cup** begins and ends with stops. Continuants, on the other hand, are produced with a continuous flow of breath. The word **sun** begins and ends with continuants. Because continuants can be said with a continuous stream of breath, they are easier to discriminate and can be pronounced in isolation with a minimum of distortion. Stops and continuants are listed in Table X.

TABLE X

Kinds of Consonants

Stops	Continuants	
/b/	/f/	/hw/
/d/	/h/	/y/
/g/	/j/	/z/
/k/	/l/	/ch/
/p/	/m/	/sh/
/t/	/n/	/th/
	/r/	/zh/
	/s/	/ŋ/
	/v/	
	/w/	

Other factors to be considered when selecting a sequence of presentation are the consonants that appear in the words students will meet and confusability. If students are going to read about Sam and Sally going sailing, then it would make sense to introduce the consonant letter **s.** Other correspondences should provide a contrast so that there will be less chance of confusing the consonants. Introducing **b, p,** and **d,** together, for example, would be potentially confusing since these letters have a similar appearance and represent similar sounds.

TEACHING CONSONANT DIGRAPHS

Consonant digraphs represent single sounds and so they are no harder to discriminate or perceive than consonants represented by single letters. However, when teaching consonant digraphs, emphasize that the two letters stand for just one sound.

TEACHING CLUSTERS

In a number of programs, clusters aren't taught. In some synthetic approaches, students are taught to sound out each letter and then blend their sounds. When the student is faced with the word **tree,** he would say /t/, /r/, /ē/ and then synthesize the sounds into /trē/. Even in analytic programs, clusters are often given short shrift. The rationale is that if a student has been introduced to initial /t/ and initial /r/, the youngster should be able to handle the cluster **tr.** Unfortunately, decoding clusters doesn't work out quite that easily. Many youngsters have difficulty with clusters. They need to be taught how to decode them.

Here is how clusters might be taught using an analytic approach. Note that auditory discrimination and perception have been merged into one step. By the time clusters are introduced, students have most likely developed adequate auditory discrimination.

Auditory Discrimination/Perception

Hold up the following objects: a star, a stamp, a stick. Have students say the name of each one. Ask: how are their names alike? What do you notice about the way their names begin? Lead students to see that the names begin with the same sound. (If necessary, point out that they begin with two sounds put together.)

Have students suggest other words that begin like **star.** Discuss why each response does or does not have the same beginning sound as **star.** Use the following miniriddles as hints if students have difficulty thinking of words that begin with **st.**

Another name for a **rock.** (stone)
A home for a horse. (stable)
Another name for **begin.** (start)
Something you like to hear. (story)
This means "don't go." (stop)

Matching Letters and Sounds

Hold up the star, stick, and stamp again. Say the name of each and write the names on the board. Remind students that the words begin with the same sound. Ask students to tell what is the same about the way the words look. Lead students to see that the words begin with the same two letters, **st.** Tell students that **st** stands for the sound heard at the beginning of **star.** Explain that the letters **st** put two sounds together, the **s** as heard at the beginning of **sun** and the **t** heard at the beginning of **tiger.** Have students read the **st** words written on the chalkboard.

Practice

• Ditto blank stars for students. Have students label the stars and then color them. Have students draw or cut out and paste on their stars pictures whose names begin like **star.** Help them to label each illustration.

• Have students complete workbook exercises that reinforce **st** = /st/ or create exercises for students. See pp. 28-31 for suggestions.

• Have students follow a series of printed commands that include **st** words: Stand, Sit, Start hopping, Stop hopping, Read a story.

• Have students make new words by adding **s** or **t** to the following: **top, till, tore, sand, say.** First, help students read the original words if they can't read them on their own.

Application

• Have students read easy stories that contain **st.**

• Help students create experience stories that contain **st** words. They may write about a talking stone or what a star sees, for example.

• Have students read real world signs that start with **st**: STOP, STEP UP, STORY HOUR.

• Have students use context and **st** to guess what words might fit in the following sentences. Accept any answer that begins with **st** and makes sense. Read the sentences if students can't read them.

1. I will read a st_____.
2. I got a gold st_____ on my paper.
3. We will go to the st_____ and buy toys.
4. It is time to st_____ playing.
5. Don't st_____ on the kitten.

ALTERNATIVE TECHNIQUES FOR PRESENTING CLUSTERS

Since a cluster is composed of letter-sound correspondences that have been taught, you might want to relate the cluster to consonant relationships that the students already know. For example, in presenting the cluster **st,** you might write the following words on the board in two separate columns.

top	say
table	sing
	sand

Have students read the words **top** and **table**. Remind them that **top** and **table** begin with the same sound. Have them suggest other words that begin like **top** and **table**. Review the fact that **t** stands for the sound heard at the beginning of **top** and **table**.

Then have students read **say, sing,** and **sand**. Give help if needed. Note that these words also begin with the same sound. Have students suggest other words that begin like **say, sing,** and **sand**. Review the fact that **s** stands for the sound heard at the beginning of **say, sing,** and **sand**.

Point to the word **top**. Tell students you would like to make the word **stop**. Ask them to tell what letter would be added to **top** to make **stop**. Then tell students you would like to make the word **stable**. Discuss briefly what a stable is. Ask what letter would be added to **table** to make **stable**. Follow this same procedure with **say, sing,** and **sand**. Have all five words read. Lead students to see that **st** stands for the sound heard at the beginning of each word. Point out that two letters have been put together to make the sound heard at the beginning of words like **stop** and **stable**.

Have students do the practice and application exercises suggested on pp. 28-31.

CONSONANT GENERALIZATIONS

Although a fairly large number of rules or generalizations have been formulated to help students assign the proper pronunciation to consonant letters, not all of these are easy to apply or have a high degree of utility. Listed below are some of the most useful generalizations. Most of these deal with problem consonants.

MOST USEFUL GENERALIZATIONS

• The letter **c** represents /k/ when followed by **a, o,** or **u: cat, cot, cut.**

• The letter **c** represents /s/ when followed by **e, i,** or **y: cent, cigar, cycle.**

• The letter **g** represents /g/ when followed by **a, o,** or **u: gas, got, gun.** The letter **g** sometimes represents /g/ when followed by **e** or **i: get, give.**

• The letter **g** often represents /j/ when followed by **e, i,** or **y: gem, giraffe, gym.**

• The letter **e** marks **c** and **g** as having /s/ and /j/ sounds when it follows **c** and **g** at the end of a word: **face, age.**

TEACHING GENERALIZATIONS

Students seem to learn best when generalizations are presented inductively. To present the **c** = /s/ and **c** = /k/ generalizations, write the following words on the board in two columns, A and B.

A	B
call	cent
catch	certain
cold	city
cup	circle
cut	cycle

Ask students what is the same about all the words. Then ask them how the words in Column A differ from the words in Column B. Lead them to see that the **c** words in Column A begin with a /k/ sound and those in Column B begin with an /s/ sound. Ask them to tell what letters follow **c** when it stands for the sound of /k/ and what letters follow **c** when it represents the sound of /s/. Help the class formulate generalizations for the /k/ sound of **c** and the /s/ sound of **c**.

Teach the **g** = /g/ and **g** = /j/ generalizations in the same way. The following words can be used as a basis for formulating the other generalizations. Keep in mind, however, that there are a number of exceptions to the generalizations.

g = /g/	**g** = /j/
game	gem
garden	germ
gate	gentle
goat	giant
good	giraffe
got	gym
gum	
guy	

E Marker

The following words might be used to illustrate the effect of **e** on **c** and **g.**

ace	age
bounce	arrange
chance	baggage
choice	cabbage
dance	cage
face	danger
ice	charge
juice	damage
nice	huge
place	large
rice	page
space	village
twice	

REINFORCEMENT ACTIVITIES

Listed below are some activities designed to provide students with added practice with consonant relationships. Adapt these to fit the particular needs of your youngsters.

Auditory Perception of Consonants

• Have students group themselves according to the beginning sounds of their names. Ben, Barbara, and Bernard would be in the /b/ group. Sammy and Cindy would be in the /s/ group. At the appropriate time, put Sammy's and Cindy's name on the board and point out that the same sound is sometimes spelled with different letters.

• Have children bring in objects whose names begin with the same sound as their names. The /b/ group might bring in a ball and some bananas, for example. Have them place their objects in bags. Have blindfolded students feel the objects and guess what they might be. Before they start guessing, remind students that the object will begin with the sound heard at the beginning of **ball.**

• Use real world materials to help teach phonics. Play consonant supermarket. Have students fill bags with cans and boxes of food or labels that contain a particular sound. For example, when studying **b** = /b/, students might put the following items in their /b/ bags: baked beans, bananas, beets, barbecue sauce, barley, and other /b/ foods. As an alternative to using boxes, cans, or labels, have students cut pictures of foods beginning with /b/ from magazines, newspaper ads, or store circulars.

Have a /b/ day. Everybody wears something that begins with /b/ and/or brings in an object that begins with /b/. Read stories that have /b/ sounds in their titles. Make students whose names begin with /b/ guests of honor.

• Play "I spy. . . ." Tell students you see something in the room that begins with the same sound as **ball**. Give a hint or two. It has a red cover. It has pages. The student who guesses that the object is a book takes over.

• Have students use *Printshop* or another graphics program to draw objects that begin with /b/.

Letter-Sound Mastery

• Have students show which letters represent beginning consonants that you say. Buy or make a set of letter cards for students. Periodically practice with three to five of the letters. For example, tell students that the class will be using the letters **t**, **s**, and **m**. Make sure students have these letters on their desks. Say words that begin with /s/, /m/, or /t/. When you say the word **soap**, students hold up the **s** card. Glance around the room to make sure students are choosing the right cards. Make a note of those who are having difficulty. Give them extra practice as needed. Use the same procedure for ending consonants. Prepare special cards for consonant clusters.

• Label all objects in the room that begin with **b**. Encourage students to read the labels.

• Have students construct a dictionary of letters and their sounds. Have them paste in or draw pictures of objects whose names begin with **b**. Help students label each picture so they see that the letter **b** represents the sound heard at the beginning of the name of each object.

• Construct a **b** bulletin board. Cut out large upper and lower case **b**s and place them on a bulletin board. Have students place on the board drawings of objects whose names begin with **b**. Label each object.

• Loan out an inexpensive Polaroid® camera. Have students photograph **b** objects. Put the photos on the bulletin board. Label each photo with its name and the name of the youngster who took it.

• Construct an initial consonant board game. Students twirl a spinner. If the board has only letters on it, students must name an object that begins with the letter shown. If it has only pictures on it, students must tell the first letter of the name of the pictured object.

• Have a series of initial consonant boxes. Have students place toys whose names begin with the appropriate letter in the boxes. Students might place a toy bike, barn, and ball in the **b** box.

• Have students look at alphabet books and identify the objects that begin with a certain letter. Have older students create alphabet books and read them to younger students.

• Have older students compose alphabet books by taking photos of real objects to illustrate keywords. For example, students might photograph a baseball to put on the **b** page. The correspondence **c** = /k/ might be accompanied by the keyword **car** and an illustration of a car.

• Compose a group experience story that uses as many **b** words as possible. The class might compose an experience story about the busy bee who bought a baseball and bat.

• Have students learn words beginning with consonants that have been taught. Construct a series of cards. Put a picture of an object on one side. Put the word that names the picture on the other. The words should be easy high-frequency words that are readily depicted: **cat, ball, man, horse.** Have youngsters check themselves by trying to read the word and then looking at the pictured side to see if they are correct. As students accumulate a number of pictured words, teach them a few sight words and have them compose sentences with their words.

• Use a Language Master or other card reader to compose initial consonant cards. The card might show and name a ball and a bat. The student tells what letter the objects begin with. The answer is recorded and the child then checks his answer with the prerecorded correct answer.

• Play consonant concentration. Have students match up picture cards whose name illustrate a particular correspondence and tell with what letter the cards begin. A student matching up two cards with buses on them would say that they begin with the letter **b.**

• Have older students find objects and services that begin with **b** in the Yellow Pages. Tell them you want to order a loaf of bread from the bakery or open a bank account. Ask them what letter you would look under in the Yellow Pages. Have students find a listing of bakeries and banks.

Consonant Substitution

• Have students change words by substituting consonants. Stress the need to create real words. For example, given the word **cat,** students substitute initial consonants to make the following words: **bat, fat, hat, mat, pat, rat,** and **sat.**

• Create sentences in which one word does not make sense but would make sense if it had a different initial consonant letter or consonant cluster. Have students change the erroneous letters. These exercises give students practice with consonant substitution and also force them to use context and read for meaning. Listed below are some sample sentences:

1. Jan has a pet hat.
2. We fat on the mat.
3. The cat fan from the dog.
4. That man is my bad.
5. Hit the ball with a rat.

Integrating Phonics with Meaning

Students should use meaning along with phonics clues as they decode words. Try using cloze or modified cloze exercises so that students learn to use language clues and the sense of the text to help them decode. Read sentences that have missing words. Give the first letter of the missing word and have students guess what the whole word might be. Some sample sentences are:

1. The b_____ rolled under the car.
2. I will ride my b_____.
3. I can read this b_____.

In using modified cloze, the options might include one or more phonics elements that have been recently introduced. For example, if the **ch** and **sh** digraphs have been recently taught, you might present sentences similar to the following:

They sailed to the new land in three _____.
(chips, sips, ships)
The dog helped the farmer care for the _____.
(sheep, seep, cheap)

Using Mnemonic Devices to Help Students Learn Consonants

Several programs use mnemonic devices to help students learn initial consonant correspondences. Both the *Laubach* and *Houghton Mifflin* reading programs use superimposed drawings to illustrate the sounds of letters. For example, *Houghton Mifflin* has a fish drawn over the letter **f** to remind students that **f** stands for the sound heard at the beginning of **fish**. The *Laubach* series has a **cup** nestled in the letter **c** to remind older learners that **c** represents the sound heard at the beginning of **cup**.

Cut up a *Houghton Mifflin* or *Laubach* workbook and create a chart of these mnemonic devices for each consonant. Or have students create and draw mnemonic illustrations for various consonants. For example, a tiger standing on hind legs with front paws outstretched might be used to illustrate the correspondence $t = /t/$.

Open Court uses a mnemonic system in which an object or action is paired with a consonant sound. The letter **m,** for example, appears on an illustration that shows a girl eating ice cream. The girl is saying "mmm" because the ice cream tastes good. This is the sound of /m/ in isolation.

Use Open Court's devices for remembering /m/ and other sounds or have students create their own. Give each sound a name. The $s = /s/$ correspondence, for example, might be labeled the hissing snake sound. In periodic drills, you say the name of the sound and have students say the sound and the letters that represent it. This technique should be especially helpful for youngsters who have difficulty remembering sound-letter associations.

CONSONANT LISTS

Included in this section are lists of words that serve as examples for the major consonant letter-sound correspondences. The words might be used for creating lessons and exercises for students. They might also be used to supply you with additional examples for elements presented in your basal series. Single-consonant correspondences are presented first. Digraphs and clusters follow.

Single Consonants

b = /b/

initial			final	
book	boat	bee	cab	Bob
boy	bat	bank	crab	cub
bird	box	board	club	tub
bus	barn	banana	web	tube
by	ball	beard	robe	tab

c = /k/

initial

cake	corn	carrot	cut	camera
cat	count	camel	cost	carpenter
coat	call	cold	candy	catcher
cow	can	color	cave	cause

c = /s/

initial		final
circle	cigar	face
cent	celery	mice
city	cement	ice
circus	center	fence
cereal	ceiling	place

d = /d/

initial			final	
dog	dime	day	bed	dad
door	done	dad	bread	road
deer	down	daughter	bird	read
duck	do	dollar	red	side
desk	dust	doctor	crowd	made

f = /f/

initial			final	
fish	fork	fat	chief	safe
five	food	far	leaf	wife
foot	fox	full	knife	if
fence	fell	fine	roof	off
farm	fast	feed	life	thief

g = /g/

initial			final	
girl	give	garage	dog	fog
goat	got	garbage	leg	rag
gate	gas	gift	bag	log
gun	gold	good	rug	mug
game	garden	guy	bug	tag

g = /j/

initial

			final	
giant	general		page	huge
gentle	gem		age	large
gerbil	genuine		cage	range
gym	germ		change	sponge
giraffe	geography		charge	stage

h = /h/

initial

hat	hen	head	hog	hamburger
house	had	heart	hide	haste
horse	hall	heat	him	hate
hand	happy	hair	hurt	howl
hill	help	here	hood	helicopter

j = /j/

initial

jet	just	jacket	jewel
jar	jelly	judge	January
jeep	joy	join	June
jump	juice	jam	July
job	junk	jaw	jungle

k = /k/

initial

key	kitchen
king	kind
kite	kangaroo
kitten	keep
kick	kid

l = /l/

initial

			final	
lock	last	ladder	nail	oil
leaf	look	light	girl	seal
lamp	like	large	owl	heel
leg	lost	laugh	pole	mail
lips	live	learn	sail	howl

m = /m/

initial			final	
main	might	meat	name	from
map	men	mark	ham	dime
moon	may	me	game	gym
monkey	maker	must	aim	gum
mat	my	mile	them	room

n = /n/

initial			final	
nail	nose	nurse	man	sun
nine	name	no	moon	rain
nickel	nut	north	can	won
neck	net	needle	fan	ten
nest	night	note	barn	chin

p = /p/

initial			final	
pen	pie	park	cup	trip
pan	put	pole	map	up
paw	part	penny	ship	tape
pool	pull	pay	soap	soup
pin	point	paste	top	keep

r = /r/

		initial		
ring	red	radio	rabbit	reason
rug	room	round	raccoon	receive
rake	road	rest	rain	record
rose	ride	real	raise	remember
rock	run	reach	rather	robot

s, se = /s/

initial			final	
sun	seat	sign	bus	base
saw	six	seed	yes	geese
sock	seven	sad	us	worse
sail	sense	sorry	this	case
seed	sea	sister	gas	horse

s, se = /z/

	final
is	rose
has	cheese
news	nose
was	chose
woods	lose

t = /t/

initial			final	
table	ten	talk	cat	not
tie	tomato	tell	boat	get
tire	take	touch	foot	coat
tent	time	turtle	it	meat
tape	turn	top	hat	note

v = /v/

initial			final	
van	very	vacation	have	live
vase	village	violin	brave	leave
vest	visit	vowel	above	love
vet	vegetable	vinegar	cave	wave
vine	value	valley	dive	believe

w = /w/

		initial		
watch	work	way	wish	warm
web	we	wet	west	week
wolf	wood	was	went	wing
window	were	walk	want	wait
win	wide	word	wild	wear

x = /ks/

	final
fox	wax
box	ax
six	fix
tax	ox
mix	relax

x = /gz/

        medial

exact	exaggerate
exam	exist
example	

y = /y/

    initial

yo-yo	yard
you	year
young	

z = /z/

initial	final
zebra	fuzz
zipper	doze
zoo	breeze
zoom	prize
zig-zag	sneeze

Clusters

L Clusters

bl = /bl/

        initial

black	blood	blur
blue	blame	bleach
blanket	blind	blade
block	blend	bleed
blink	blouse	bloom

cl = /cl/

        initial

clock	clean	clump
clown	clay	clutch
club	claw	clothes
cloth	clear	clarinet
climb	cloud	clever

fl = /fl/

initial

flag	flake	flew
floor	flame	flavor
flower	flip	flee
fly	flap	flick
flat	flash	front

gl = /gl/

initial

glove
glass
glad
glow
glue

-ld = /ld/

final

child	told
cold	field
gold	hold
wild	build
old	sold

-lf = /lf/

final

elf
shelf
himself
herself
wolf

-lt = /lt/

final

belt	felt
salt	built
colt	fault
bolt	quilt
melt	halt

pl = /pl/

  initial

plate	please
plow	play
plant	plum
plan	plenty
place	plain

R Clusters

br = /br/

   initial

bread	breakfast	broom
brick	bright	brook
brown	bring	brush
bridge	broke	brave
brother	branch	breath

cr = /cr/

   initial

crayon	crash	crane
crib	crawl	crocodile
cross	creep	crew
crack	crow	crop
crab	cricket	cruel

dr = /dr/

  initial

dress	dry
drum	dragon
drop	drain
draw	drink
drive	drizzle

fr = /fr/

  initial

frog	from
fruit	friend
free	frame
fry	freeze
front	fresh

gr = /gr/

    initial

grape	great
grass	grandfather
green	grandmother
gray	ground
grow	growl

pr = /pr/

    initial

price	practice
prize	principal
print	prove
pretty	prince
present	pretzel

-rd = /rd/

                                    final

bird	hard
board	third
yard	guard
beard	heard
word	sword

-rk = /rk/

                                      final

fork	shark
mark	spark
park	cork
dark	pork
lark	work

-rm = /rm/

                                      final

arm	term
farm	form
warm	germ
worm	storm
harm	squirm

-rn = /rn/

final	
barn	turn
corn	torn
born	worn
horn	learn
burn	earn

-rt = /rt/

final	
heart	court
cart	dart
fort	port

S Clusters

sc = /sk/

initial

scale	scold
scar	score
scatter	scooter
scarf	scout
scare	scuff

scr = /skr/

initial

screen
scrap
scrape
scratch
scream

shr = /shr/

initial

shrimp	shrug
shrink	shriek
shred	shrill
shrub	shrunk
shrine	shrivel

sk = /sk/

initial		final
skunk	skin	desk
skirt	skinny	ask
sky	skate	mask
ski	skid	disk
skip	skill	task

sl = /sl/

initial

sled	sleeve
sleep	slap
slam	slant
slip	slipping
slow	sly

sm = /sm/

initial

smile	smart
smoke	smack
small	smash
smell	smear
smooth	smudge

sn = /sn/

initial

snake	snow
snail	sneeze
sneakers	sniff
snack	snooze
snap	snip

sp = /sp/

initial   final

spider	spank		wasp
spoon	spark		grasp
spot	spinach		crisp
space	spend		clasp
spin	spoke		

spr = /spr/

initial

spring
spray
sprinkle
spread
sprung

st = /st/

initial   final

star	stop	steel	nest	fast
stamp	start	stir	test	most
stick	still	state	list	must
stone	stood	sting	last	least
step	stay	station	dust	just

str = /str/

initial

strawberry	strike
string	strange
stream	straight
street	strict
strong	stripe

squ = /skw/

initial

squirrel	squash
square	squeeze
squeak	squirm
squawk	squid
squirt	squint

sw = /sw/

initial

sweater	sweet
sweep	swallow
swell	switch
swim	swam
swing	sweat

Other Clusters

mp = /mp/

final

lamp	camp	shrimp
damp	limp	skimp
jump	pump	swamp
bump	stamp	thump
dump	stump	tramp

nd = /nd/

final

hand	and	send
end	round	band
sand	find	land
found	wind	ground
second	bend	sound

nt = /nt/

final

tent	point
ant	went
cent	front
plant	aunt
mint	count

nk = /ŋk/

final

bank	think
skunk	blink
ink	pink
sank	crank
tank	stink

nce = /ns/

final

since	fence
once	dance
prince	chance

qu = /kw/

initial

queen	quart
question	quarrel
quack	quarter
quick	quit
quiet	quite

tw = /tw/

initial

twelve	twine
twig	twinkle
twin	twenty
twice	twirl
twist	twitch

Digraphs

ch = /ch/

	initial			final	
chair	chin	chink		peach	rich
church	children	chuckle		beach	ranch
chest	cheer	chip		lunch	bunch
chief	chimney	chew		bench	each
chicken	choose	cheek		branch	inch

ch = /k/

initial

chemical
character
chorus
choir
chrome

ch = /sh/

initial	medial	final
chef	machine	mustache
Chicago		
chauffeur		

ck = /k/

	final	
lock	back
trunk	black
rock	neck
clock	thick
stick	quick

dge = /j/

	final	
bridge	lodge
judge	pledge
edge	smudge
ledge	wedge
fudge	knowledge

gh = /f/

final
enough
laugh
rough
tough
graph

kn = /n/

initial

knee	know
knife	knot
knit	knob
knew	knock
knuckle	kneel

ng = /ŋ/

final

king	bring
ring	wrong
sting	thing
sing	strong
song	young

sh = /sh/

initial			final	
ship	shell	shout	fish	fresh
sheep	shin	should	wish	hush
shoe	shore	shop	dish	crash
she	short	shoulder	wash	leash
show	shirt	share	push	squash

sc = /s/

initial
science
scissors
scene
scent
scientist

ph = /f/

initial

phone
photo
phonics
phony
pheasant

th = /th/

initial		final
the	them	bathe
then	they	breathe
this	those	mouth (v.)
there	than	with
that	though	smooth

th = /th/ voiceless

initial		final
thumb	thank	bath
thin	they	cloth
thorn	thief	earth
third	think	tooth
thick	thing	path

t = /ch/

initial

picture	adventure
feature	capture
nature	creature
future	fortune
actual	mixture

tch = /ch/

final

catch	stretch
crutch	switch
ditch	watch
patch	match
scratch	pitch

ti = /ch/

initial

question
mention
attention
essential
exhaustion

ti = /sh/

initial

addition	action
condition	motion
position	direction
nation	section
patient	station

wh = /(h)w/[1]

initial

wheel	wheat
what	while
when	which
where	whip
whale	white

wh = /h/

initial

who
whose
whom
whole
whomever

wr = /r/

initial

wrist	wreath
write	wreck
wrap	wrench
wrong	wring
wrote	wrestle

Footnote

1. Depending on dialect, many **wh** words are pronounced /hw/ or /w/.

CHAPTER IV

TEACHING VOWEL RELATIONSHIPS

LIKE CONSONANTS, vowels are also taught in three main ways: through presentation within the context of a word, in isolation, and through contrasting patterns. Eclectic basals present vowels analytically, in the context of a whole word. However, unlike consonants, vowels may be presented in isolation without distortion. Phonics-first programs usually introduce vowels in isolation. Linguistic programs present vowels through contrasting patterns.

USING AN ANALYTIC APPROACH TO TEACH VOWELS

Generally, vowels are introduced in a five-part lesson that includes: auditory discrimination, auditory perception, linking of letter-sound relationships, practice, and application. Here is how a short **a** would be introduced in an analytic approach.

Auditory Discrimination

Auditory discrimination of vowels presented in the context of a word may be slightly more difficult than discrimination of consonants since most vowels occur in the middle of words so students are often distinguishing between medial rather than initial sounds. To develop auditory discrimination, present the following activities, which force students to distinguish between similar sounding words.

Activity 1: Hold up the following real objects or pictures and ask:

(Holding up a pan) Is this a pan or a pen?
(Holding up a bag) Is this a bag or a bug?
(Holding up a cup) Is this a cap or a cup?

(Holding up a toy cat or picture of a cat) Is this a cat or a cut?
(Holding up a pot) Is this a pot or a pat?
(Holding up a tack) Is this a tick or a tack?
(Holding up a picture of a ham) Is this a ham or a home?
(Holding up a picture of a van) Is this a van or a vine?
(Holding up a can) Is this a can or a cane?
(Holding up a map) Is this a map or a mop?

This first activity was suggested by Hillerich and Johnson's work (1986). See their program for additional activities of this type.

Activity 2: Say the following word pairs. Have students tell if you are saying the same word twice or two different words. To get a response from the whole class, have students raise both hands if the words are the same but just one hand if they are different.

List 1		List 2	
bake	book	hat	hit
cap	cape	pan	pen
lad	load	had	had
cat	Kate	cat	cat
ham	home	rat	rat
pan	pan	at	it
Sam	same	map	mop
ran	rain	fan	fin
tap	tape	bat	bit
sat	suit	ax	ox

Auditory Perception

Activity 1: Hold up a series of objects or illustrations of objects: a hat, pan, bag, and map, for example. Have students name each object. Then repeat the name of each object and ask students to tell what is the same about the name of each object. Ask: How are the names of **hat, pan, bag,** and **map** the same? Discuss with students the fact that **hat, pan, bag,** and **map** have the same sound in the middle.

Activity 2: Have students stand up if their first names have the same sound as that heard in the middle of **hat**: Pat, Ann, Matt, Andrew, Sam, etc.

Activity 3: Play animal riddles. Tell students that the names of the animals must have the same sound as is heard in the middle of **hat.**

Some sample riddles include:

I have wings.
But I am not a bird.
I look like a mouse. (bat)

Cats chase me.
People try to get rid of me.
I eat garbage and trash. (rat)

A lot of people have me for a pet.
I can't sing.
And I can't bark.
But I can purr. (cat)

Linking of Letter and Sound

Write **pan, hat, bag,** and **map** on the board in a single column. Say and spell each word as you write it on the board. Then read all the words again, pointing to each one as you pronounce it. Remind students that each word has the same middle sound. Ask: What letter is the same in all of these words? Explain that the letter **a** makes the sound heard in the middle of each of the words. Read the words once more, underlining the letter **a** in each as you do so. Tell students that the letter **a** is a vowel letter. Explain that vowel letters may stand for a number of different sounds, but that in these words the vowel letter **a** stands for the sound heard in the middle of **hat.** Have students say **hat,** listening for the vowel sound in the middle of the word as they do so. Have volunteers read the short **a** words that have been placed on the board.

Practice

• Have students read, with your help, sentences containing short **a** words or compose an experience story using short **a** words. Students might write a story about a cat who sees a rat, for example.

• Compose a series of words that contain short **a** and initial and final consonants that students have learned. Help students use their knowledge of short **a** and the consonants to decode the words.

• Complete workbook exercises that deal with short **a**, if these are appropriate and useful, or create practice exercises and games of your own.

• Have students complete fill-in-the-blank exercises that contain short **a** words. If students have learned other short vowel correspondences, construct the exercises in such a way that students contrast short **a** words with other short vowel words. For example, if students have already been introduced to short **i**, you might present the following exercise.

Underline the word that makes better sense in each sentence.

1. Put on your (hat, hit).
2. You may (sat, sit).
3. Put your things in a (bag, big).
4. See if you can (hat, hit) the ball.
5. My dog is (tan, tin) and white.

• Label objects in your room that contain short **a** (map, plant, bat, lamp). Encourage students to read the labels. After a few days, remove the labels from the objects and see if students can read the labels.

• Display food products that contain labels that have a short **a** (canned ham, apples, Apple Jacks, tea bags). Encourage students to read the labels.

Application

• Encourage students to use context and their knowledge of short **a** to decode unfamiliar short **a** words.

• Have students read stories in their reading series that contain short **a**.

• Encourage students to read easy books that contain short **a**. (See "Children's Books That Can Be Used to Reinforce Word Attack Skills" in Chapter XI for a listing of books of this type.)

USING A SYNTHETIC APPROACH TO INTRODUCE VOWELS

A synthetic or sound-by-sound approach also employs five steps to introduce vowels. The main difference between the synthetic and analytic approaches is that the vowel is pronounced in isolation in the synthetic approach. In the analytic approach it is pronounced in the context of a word. Pronouncing the vowel in isolation is not a negative feature. Unlike consonants, vowels can be pronounced in isolation without distortion. Vowels presented in isolation would be easier to discriminate and perceive. Here is how short **a** might be presented in a synthetic approach.

Auditory Discrimination

This step would be identical to the presentation in the analytic approach.

Auditory Perception

Tell students to listen as you say the words **ax, ant, apple.** Lead students to see that they all begin with the same sound. Explain that the words begin with the sound /a/.

Say the words listed below. If a word has the sound /a/, the students raise their hands. If a word does not have an /a/ sound, the students do not raise their hands.

apple	hat	bag	pat
cat	dad	pan	ten
box	man	cap	run
fan	fun	pig	nap
sun	rag	way	can

Linking of Letter-Sound Relationships

Write **apple, ant,** and **ax** on the board. Read the words as you write them. Lead students to see that each word begins with the letter **a.** Tell students that the letter **a** is a vowel letter and that vowel letters may stand for more than one sound. Tell them that one sound the letter **a** stands for is /a/. Have students listen for the sound of /a/ as you read the words once more. Then have volunteers read the words.

Practice/Application

Practice and application activities would be the same as those presented for the analytic approach.

USING A LINGUISTIC APPROACH TO TEACH VOWELS

A linguistic approach depends on the students' ability to compare and contrast in order to learn vowel correspondence. These are the main steps of a linguistic introduction of short **a** as summarized from the *Merrill Linguistic Readers* (Wilson and Rudolph, 1980).

The teacher writes the word **cat** on the board. She says the word, points to each letter as she spells it, and then uses the word in an oral sentence. The students say the word and use it in oral sentences.

The word **fat** is written directly underneath the word **cat,** is spelled, and used in an oral sentence. Students are asked to tell what differences they see between the word **fat** and the word **cat.** The word **Nat** is then introduced and contrasted. The students read all three words. The words are then read in sentences that have been written on the chalkboard.

Students read and spell the pattern words in their readers. Students also read patterns in which the order of the words has been changed. To apply their knowledge of the patterns, students read stories containing the pattern words.

USING A WORD BUILDING APPROACH

The simplest, most direct way to present both vowels and consonants is through building words. Although it deals with individual letters and sounds, this approach does not involve any distortion of sounds and works especially well with students who are having difficulty perceiving and learning letter-sound relationships.

The approach begins with a vowel since the vowel is the core of a word. It may be started with short vowels, but long vowels are recommended for initial instruction since they are easy to perceive, and a number of easy-to-read, high-frequency words can be formed with just two sounds. Here is how the approach works.

Step 1: Introducing the Letter-Sound Relationship

Write the letter **o** on the chalkboard. Ask: "Can anyone tell me the name of this letter? Yes, this is the letter **o.** The letter **o** sometimes stands for the sound /ō/. Now you say /ō/." (Point to the letter **o** as the students say its sound.) "We call this the long sound of **o.**"

Step 2: Building Words

Tell students: "I want to make a word with the letter **o.** I want to make the word **no.** What letter would I add to **o** to make the word **no?**" Show students how the letter **n** is added to **o** to make **no.** Have several students read the word.

Form other words in the same way. Write **o** under the word **no**. Ask students what letter would have to be added to make **go**. Write another **o** under **go** and have the word **so** formed. Have each of the words read and used in oral sentences.

Step 3: Practice/Application

• Complete workbook exercises using the correspondence **o** = /ō/ or create exercises of your own.

• Create experience stories that use the correspondence. Students might write a story about the day there was no gas and the cars would not go.

• Read signs and other real-world materials that contain the correspondence (No Pets, No Parking).

• Read stories in basal readers and trade books that contain the correspondence.

Step 4: Extension

Lead students to see that long **o** may be spelled in a number of ways. Introduce other high-frequency spellings of long **o**: **ow, o-e, oa**.

Presenting Short Vowels

When introducing short vowels using the word building approach, follow a slightly different procedure. In teaching short **o**, for example, follow these steps: Write the word **no** on the board. Have students tell what sound the letter represents in the word **no** (long **o**) and have them form several long **o** words (**go, so**). Then tell them that when a letter is placed after it, **o** can represent another sound. Tell students that you want to write /ot/. Write **o** on the board. Place a **t** after the **o** and tell students that the letter **o** now stands for /o/ and the letters **o** and **t** stand for /ot/.

Then tell students that you want to make the word **not**. Have them tell what letter would be placed before /ot/ to make **not**. Have several students read the word **not** and use it in oral sentences. Have other -ot words formed in the same way (**got, hot, pot, rot**). Practice and application activities will be the same as those for long vowels.

SEQUENCE OF TEACHING VOWELS

No words can exist without a vowel. However, vowels are often taught after some or most of the consonants have been introduced. In some programs, vowels are not taught until the middle of the first grade or even later. The reasoning behind the delayed introduction of vowels is that vowel spellings are more variable than consonant spellings, and consonants are more useful than vowels in decoding unfamiliar words (Marchbanks and Levin, 1965). Students are taught to use consonants and context as their major word attack strategies.

In phonics-first programs, vowels are introduced along with consonants or after just three or four consonants have been taught. Stories are composed of words that contain letter-sound relationships that have already been taught. Students are then able to use their knowledge of consonant and vowel letter-sound relationships to decode words. A student taught by a synthetic phonics-first program faced with the unfamiliar word **pet** would say "puh-eh-tuh: pet." A student taught by an analytic method would use the sound represented by the initial consonant and context to decode **pet**.

In both phonics-first and analytic programs, short vowels are generally introduced before long vowels. Short vowel sounds have fewer spellings and are found in more words. Short vowels generally have one major spelling whereas long vowels may have two or three main spellings. Short **a**, for example, is most often spelled **a** as in **hat**. Long **a**, on the other hand, is often spelled **a-e** as in **hate**, **ay/ai** as in **ray** and **raisin,** or **a** at the end of a syllable as in **radar**.

Based on the theory that long vowels are easier to perceive, some phonics-first programs, such as *Keys to Reading* (Matteoni, Sucher, Klein, & Welch, 1986) and Open Court's *Headway* program (Carus, 1985), do teach long vowels before introducing short vowels. *Headway* starts its program with the long **e**. Students form words by adding the consonants **m**, **p,** and t to various spellings of long **e**.

Keys to Reading, one of the most popular phonics-first programs, begins its program by introducing two spellings of long **o**: **o-e** as in **rope** and **oa** as in **boat**.

Although variability of spelling and ease of perception are important considerations in creating a sequence of instruction, frequency of occurrence also needs to be taken into account when deciding the order in which vowel correspondences should be introduced. If everything else is equal, sequence should probably be determined on the basis of frequency. Listed in Table XI are the twenty most frequently occurring vowel correspondences (Gunning, 1975).

TABLE XI

Rank Order of Vowel Correspondences

i = /i/	y = /ē/	ee = /ē/
e = /ə/	e = /i/	o = /aw/
e = /e/	o = /o/	ea = /ē/
a = /a/	o = /ō/	i-e = /ī/
o = /ə/	i = /ī/	i = /ə/
a = /ə/	a = /ā/	a-e = /ā/
u = /ə/	a = /o/	

VOWEL GENERALIZATIONS

Although vowels are more variable in their spellings than consonants, there are a number of generalizations that can be drawn about vowel correspondences. There are two kinds of generalizations: primary and secondary. Primary generalizations are those which apply to one vowel letter (**no, hat**). Secondary generalizations encompass two vowel letters (**paid, neat**). Overall, primary vowel generalizations are more predictable.

Primary Vowel Generalizations

Short Vowel or Closed Syllable Generalization

A vowel is short when followed by a consonant or consonant cluster: **bat, winner**. The closed syllable generalization is so named because it occurs in words or syllables that end in a consonant.

The pattern applies to both single-syllable and polysyllabic words. One problem with using the generalization to decode multisyllabic words is that the reader would have to know exactly where to divide a word before he or she could decode it. To avoid this difficulty, students might be given the following generalization to apply when decoding multisyllablic words: A vowel in a beginning or middle syllable is often short if the vowel is followed by two or more consonants: **letter, batter**.

The closed syllable generalization is one of the most useful. About 40 percent of the words in the English language have a short vowel, and the generalization has a high degree of regularity, especially in single-syllable words.

Open Syllable Generalization

A vowel is long when it comes at the end of the word or syllable: **he, locate**.

This generalization also applies to both single-syllable and polysyllabic words. It occurs in a large number of words and is highly consistent in single-syllable words. However, there are a large number of exceptions in multisyllabic words. This is especially true in unaccented syllables. Unaccented syllables, because of reduced stress, often have a short vowel or schwa pronunciation. For example, the long **e** of **be** becomes a short **i** in the first syllable of **between** because the first syllable is not accented. In the word **alone,** the **a** represents a schwa sound because it is in an unaccented syllable.

As with the closed syllable generalization, the open syllable generalization may be applied without indicating exact syllable divisions. For ease of application, you might give students the following generalization: A vowel in a beginning or middle syllable is often long if followed by just one consonant: **pilot, music.**

Although not as consistent or frequent as the closed syllable generalization, the open syllable generalization is important and allows readers to distinguish between words such as **later** and **latter.**

Final e Marker Generalization

A vowel is long when followed by a consonant and a final **e** marker: **tape, note.** This generalization also applies when two consonants occur between the vowel and the final **e: change.**

The **e** marker generalization only applies slightly more than half the time. However, numerous words contain the pattern, so it is a useful generalization.

Unstressed Syllable Generalization

A vowel is given a schwa pronunciation when it occurs in an unaccented syllable: **about, tomato.**

Unaccented syllables occur in just about every multisyllabic word, so this generalization has a high frequency. It also has a fairly high percentage of exceptions. The generalization is difficult for youngsters to apply since it necessitates a knowledge of accents.

SECONDARY VOWEL GENERALIZATIONS

Secondary vowels (**ea, ai, ou**) occur less frequently than primary vowels do. Approximately, 20 percent of English words have a secondary vowel (Gunning, 1975). In the past, secondary vowels have been covered by the two-vowels generalizations: When two vowels go walking, the first one does the talking. This little rhyme was composed to remind youngsters that when two vowel letters are written next to each other, the first one represents a long sound. In the word **boat**, for example, the secondary vowel **oa** stands for a long **o**. As stated, this generalization has limited applicability because there are a large number of exceptions: **friend, steak.**

There are more than 60 letter-sound correspondences involving secondary vowels. Some of these occur rarely: **ey**=/ā/ (**they**), **ai**=/ī/ (**aisle**). Others occur with great frequency and consistency: **ee**=/ē/ (**tree**), **ay**=/ā/ (**pay**). Instead of teaching secondary vowels as a single generalization, it would make more sense to present only the most frequently occurring and consistent secondary vowel correspondences. Listed in Table XII are high frequency secondary vowel correspondences and a percentage of applicability for each one. The percentage of applicability indicates the proportion of instances in which a correspondence represents a particular sound. For example, **ai** represents the long sound of **a** about three-quarters of the time. About one time out of four it will represent a short vowel or other sound.

TABLE XII
Applicability of Secondary Vowel Correspondences

Correspondence	Percentage of Applicability	Correspondence	Percentage of Applicability
ai=/ā/	74%	ie=/ī/	25%
ar=/ar/	76%	igh=/ī/	100%
aw=/aw/	100%	oa=/ō/	100%
ay=/ā/	85%	oi=/oi/	100%
ea=/ē/	54%	oo=/o͞o/	41%
ea=/e/	23%	oo=/o͝o/	45%
ea=/i/	15%	ou=/ow/	66%
ee=/ē/	96%	ou=/ə/	32%
ei=/ē/	40%	ough=/o/	50%
ew=/o͞o/	86%	ough=/u/	31%
ey=/ē/	99%	ow=/ō/	65%
ie=/ē/	66%	ow=/ow/	35%

Major Secondary Vowel Correspondences

Described below are secondary vowels that occur with a high degree of frequency.

Correspondences

ai/ay. The letters **ai** and **ay** frequently stand for a long a sound: **pay, paid.** The digraphs **ai** and **ay** are in complementary distribution. Distribution refers to the part of the word where a letter or letter combination may occur. The letters **ai** are found in the beginning or middle of a word but may not occur at the end of a word: **aid.** The combination **ay** complements **ai** because it can be written at the end of a word: **hay, day.**

au/aw. The letters **au** and **aw** stand for the sound heard at the beginning of **author** and the end of **paw** with a high degree of consistency. The digraphs **au** and **aw** are also in complementary distribution. The letters **au** may appear in the beginning or middle of a word but not at the end. The letters **aw** may appear at the end or beginning of a word: **awful, law.**

ea. The letters **ea** most often stand for long **e** as in **team** but may also stand for short **e** as in **bread** or short **i** as in **fear.** Less frequently, **ea** represents /ə/ as in **heard** or /ā/ as in **great.**

ee. The letters **ee** almost always stand for long **e** as in **see.**

ei/ey. The letters **ei** and **ey**, which are in complementary distribution, often stand for the long **e** sound as in **receive** and **money.** Less frequently, the letters **ei** and **ey** represent long **a** as in **vein** and **obey.**

ew. The letters **ew** almost always stand for /o͞o/ or /ū/ as in **flew** and **few.**

ie. The digraph **ie** most often stands for the long **e** sound heard in **chief** or the long **i** sound heard in **lie.**

igh. The letters **igh** stand for the long **i** sound heard in **night.**

oa. The diagraph **oa** usually stands for the long **o** sound heard in **boat.**

oi/oy. The digraphs **oi/oy** stand for the /oi/ sound heard in **boil** and **boy** and are in complementary distribution.

oo. The digraph **oo** usually stands for the short double **o** sound heard in **book** or the long double **o** sound heard in **soon.**

ou/ow. The digraphs **ou** and **ow**, which are in complementary distribution, often stand for the sound of /ow/ as heard in **out** and **town.**

ou. The digraph **ou** often stands for the short **u** (schwa) sound heard in **would.**

ough. The letter combination **ough** most frequently represents long o as in **though** or long double o as in **group**.

ow. The digraph **ow** often stands for the long o sound heard in **snow**.

Flexibility in Using Secondary Vowels

Students need to be taught to be flexible when decoding words that contain secondary vowels or digraphs. Since several digraphs represent two or more sounds, students should try one pronunciation and see if they have created a real word and if that real word makes sense in context. If the word does not seem like a real word or if the word does not fit the context, students should try another frequently occurring pronunciation. For example, the digraph **oo** represents /o͞o/ or /o͝o/ 96 percent of the time. If a student came across the word **shook** and pronounced it /sho͞ok/, the student should try the /o͝o/ pronunciation because /sho͞ok/ is not a real word. Using the context of the sentence, "I **shook** the box to see if I could tell what was inside," would help the student verify that the /o͝o/ pronunciation is correct because /sho͝ok/ fits the sense of the sentence.

Teaching Vowel Generalizations

Closed Syllable Generalization

As with consonant generalizations, teach vowel generalizations inductively. To present the closed syllable generalization, for example, write the following words on the chalkboard.

at	pet	hit	hot	bus
hand	tell	will	top	run
nap	red	lip	rock	jump

Have students read the words. Lead them to see that all the words have short vowels. Also help them discover that all the words end in a consonant or consonant cluster. Help the class formulate the generalization that says that words that end in consonants usually have short vowels.

To illustrate the application of this generalization to multisyllabic words, put the words below on the chalkboard and have students read them. Lead them to see that a vowel is short if it occurs in a syllable that ends in a consonant or cluster. For beginning or medial syllables, you might point out that the vowel tends to be short if followed by two or more consonants. This eliminates the necessity of determining the exact point of syllable division.

chapter	silver
captain	cotton
pepper	follow
question	supper
sister	public

E Marker Generalization

Place the following words on the chalkboard.

A	B
can	cane
pet	Pete
bit	bite
hop	hope
us	use

Have students read the words and tell what the difference is between Columns A and B. Lead them to see that the words in Column A have short vowels and those in Column B have long vowels. Ask students to tell what letter marks the vowel in each word in Column B as being long. Tell students that **e** at the end of a word is known as a marker because it often marks vowels as being long. Help students formulate a generalization that says that a vowel that is followed by a consonant and a final **e** is often long.

Open Syllable Generalization

Place the following words on the chalkboard.

no	paper
go	even
he	tiger
me	hotel
we	future

Have the words read. Discuss the fact that they all contain long vowels. Examine the structure of the words and help students formulate the generalization that if a word or syllable ends in a vowel, the vowel is often long. For beginning or medial syllables, you might point out that the vowel is frequently long if followed by just one consonant.

REINFORCEMENT ACTIVITIES

Listed below are some activities designed to provide students with added practice with vowel relationships. Adapt these to fit the particular needs of your youngsters. The long **e** sound has been used to illustrate examples of activities. However, the activities may be used with any sound.

• Obtain labels that contain spellings of the vowel sound(s) you are currently working with. For example, if your class is working with the spellings of long **e,** use the labels from the following products: green beans, meat, beets, cheese, tea, bleach, peaches, peas. Have students read and discuss the labels. If practical, have students bring in labels from home or pictures of labels from a newspaper or magazine.

• Have students give the names of animals and insects that have the sound of long **e** in their names: **eagle, sheep, seal, flea, bee, monkey, turkey.** Create a bulletin board entitled "Long **e** Beasts." Include photos or drawings of long **e** beasts along with their names.

• Have a long **e** day. Have students bring in an object whose name contains long **e.** Objects such as the following might be brought in: bead, wheel, tea, tee (golf), key, peach, toy jeep, toy beast, toy teeth, sewing needle. Discuss each object and write its name on the board. Arrange a display of the objects. Make a label for each object so students can practice reading long **e** words.

• Obtain real signs or replicas of signs that contain long **e** words. Some possibilities include:

Main Street
Keep off the Grass
Keep to the Right
Deep Water
East 84

• Create signs for the room that incorporate long **e** words. Some possible signs are:

Free Reading Corner
No Eating in the Room
Keep Fish Tanks Clean
This Week's Meals

• Write announcements or notices that contain long **e** words. Some possible items are:

We will plant three packs of seeds this week.
There will be peaches for lunch today.
The teachers will have a meeting today.
Dr. Jones will show you how to brush your teeth.

• Have students draw a mean beast and compose a brief story about the beast.

• Have each student tell the name of the street on which she or he lives. Write the street names on the chalkboard and point to the word **street** each time it is said.

• Call attention to long **e** words that appear in content area books. For example, **east** and **tepee** might be found in a social studies text.

• Relate spelling to reading. Help students learn to spell some long **e** words that they are likely to use in their writing.

• Have students draw or collect pictures of objects whose names contain long **e**. Help them label the pictures.

• Have students create a set of word cards for long **e** words. The long **e** word can be placed on one side. The other side would contain a drawing of the word. Some long **e** words that can be depicted include the following:

knee	tea	leaf	key
three	queen	sea	peas
tree	green	peach	meat
street	seed	bean	teacher
jeep	wheel	jeans	eagle
bee	feet	seal	beast

• Teach major homophones that contain different spellings of long **e**. A sampling of long **e** homophones appears below.

be, bee	meat, meet
beach, beech	peace, piece
cheap, cheep	peak, peek
creak, creek	real, reel
heal, heel	sea, see

• Using sentences similar to the following, have students fill in the blank with the correct homophone.

1. I (sea, see) my cat.
2. Its cut will soon (heal, heel).
3. It got hurt a (weak, week) ago.
4. My cat likes (meat, meet).
5. My cat once ran after a (be, bee).

• Have students compose sentences that contain both versions of a homophone.

I felt weak all week.

The cut on my heel took a long time to heal.

• Have students answer **yes** or **no** to a series of questions that contain long **e** words.

1.	Can a seal be in the sea?	yes — no
2.	Can you eat a peach?	yes — no
3.	Can a green bean see?	yes — no
4.	Do sheep have teeth?	yes — no
5.	Can an eagle sleep?	yes — no

• Give students words that contain one vowel letter but which may be changed to represent a long **e** sound if a second vowel letter is added to form a digraph. Some words that might be so changed include the following:

at	met
set	stem
bed	bet
best	Ben
chap	red
hat	Ned
men	Jen

• To encourage the use of context, have students add a letter to change the word that doesn't make sense in each of the following sentences. Have students use a word processing program to insert letters if one is available.

1. Take a set right here.
2. It is cold. Turn the hat on.
3. What does this word men?
4. Did you red that story?
5. I have a new pair of jans.

• When working with short vowels, have students make new words by changing the medial vowel. Explain to students that they must create real words.

hat — hot, hit, hut
cat — cut, cot
bat — bet, bit, but

tap—tip, top
ham—him, hum
fan—fin, fun
lack—lick, lock, luck
lamp—limp, lump
sing—sang, song, sung

• Have students put scrambled sentences containing long **e** words in order.

1. read   I   to   like.
2. are   bees   the   tree   in?
3. beach   we   to   go   will   the.

• Have students fill in the blanks with long **e** words that fit the sense of the sentence.

1. Don't go west. Go _____.
2. I like the color _____ best.
3. Did you _____ my apple?
4. I will _____ you after school.
5. Did a _____ sting you?

• The best way to reinforce phonics elements is to have students read stories and books that contain those elements. Once students have progressed beyond the initial stages of reading, almost any book which they can handle will reinforce all the major phonic elements that have been presented. See "Children's Books That Can Be Used to Reinforce Word Attack Skills" in Chapter XI for a listing of books that reinforce specific correspondences while youngsters are in the beginning stages of learning to read. For example, one book listed is *The Foot Book* by Dr. Seuss (Random House, 1968), which might be used to provide practice with the **ee** spelling of long **e**.

VOWEL LISTS

Included in this section are lists of words that serve as examples for the major vowel letter-sound correspondences. The lists might be used for creating lessons and exercises for students, or they might be used to supply you with additional words to illustrate your vowel lessons.

Short Vowels

a = /a/

apple	cat	map	track	happen	after
ant	man	land	grass	faster	answer
ax	bag	past	stand	castle	animal
an	gas	fact	plant	captain	angry
add	lamp	glass	hand	family	action

e = /e/

ten	jet	guess	lettuce	president
bell	hen	fresh	effort	yesterday
nest	tell	spend	effect	membership
bed	pen	length	empty	television
desk	red	tent	letter	secretary

ea = /e/

bread	health	heavy	deaf	breath
instead	dead	dread	measure	meant
feather	pleasant	thread	spread	treasure

i = /i/

six	in	miss	wing	insect	continue
fish	is	ring	skin	income	discover
ship	if	will	rich	instead	principal
big	it	with	drink	itself	particular
win	it	did	quick	inside	considerate

y = /i/

gym	system	cylinder	gyp
physical	hypnotize	symbol	mystery
cymbal	syllable	rhythm	sympathize

e = /i/

enjoy	believe	between	despite	remember
except	demand	beneath	begin	determine
entire	explain	belong	prevent	develop
example	remain	responsible	degree	requirement
exciting	became	replied	design	department
remove	decide			

o = /o/

fox	top	shop	object	accomplish
pot	box	drop	offer	colony
got	cot	rock	dollar	hospital
job	pop	stop	promise	responsible
not	dot	clock	bottle	monument

a = /o/

swan	yacht	squash	swallow	wand
waffle	wash	wallet	watch	wander

u = /u/

bus	just	umpire	uncle	sun
truck	umbrella	sudden	but	lunch
number	public	run	must	summer
subway	cut	much	plumber	unhappy

o, o-e, ou = /u/

front	come	other	young
son	some	brother	double
won	above	money	enough
does	glove	monkey	county
	none		company

Long Vowels

a = /ā/

apron	paper	nature	tornado	application
April	table	later	potato	operation
able	lady	nation	volcano	education
	baby	station	tomato	stadium
	lazy	famous	favorite	radiator

a-e = /ā/

ape	name	plate	became	abbreviate
age	game	plane	exchange	graduate
ate	lake	shape	baseball	behave
ace	place	date	statement	appreciate
ache	race	wave	indicate	locate

ai = /ā/

aid	tail	claim	afraid	failure
aim	wail	faint	complain	obtain
nail	gain	paid	contain	entertain
train	plain	grain	detail	maintenance
rain	paint	strain	exclaim	remainder

e = /ē/

he	equal	meter	abbreviate	obedient
me	even	zebra	reappear	encyclopedia
we	legal	recent	adhesive	immediate
be	frequent	fever	appreciate	ingredient
she	secret	prefix	comedian	previous

e-e = /ē/

these	concrete	evening
scene	complete	trapeze
eve	extreme	athlete
scheme	stampede	compete
theme	supreme	centipede

ea = /ē/

eagle	leave	speak	beneath	feature
peach	reach	steam	season	increase
leaf	heat	wheat	treatment	measles
jeans	mean	league	beacon	reason
tea	real	stream	defeat	disease

ee = /ē/

bee	seem	steel	asleep	agreed
knee	feel	speech	between	degree
wheel	feed	street	indeed	coffee
tree	keep	sheet	fourteen	agreement
three	need	speed	freedom	committee

ei = /ē/

ceiling	receive
receipt	either
neither	

ie = /ē/

field	yield
chief	piece
brief	niece
priest	believe
thief	achieve

y = /ē/

busy	many	early	suddenly	opportunity
study	lady	hungry	completely	dictionary
very	carry	every	property	variety
body	ready	angry	library	ordinary
any	story	slowly	finally	ability

i = /ē/

radio	material	serious	interior
period	previous	various	obvious
easier	association		

i = /ī/

I	diver	climate	dinosaur	vibrations
tiger	diner	triangle	library	vitamin
spider	ivy	rifle	microscope	lion
silent	pirate	rival	scientist	dial
final	private	silent	supervisor	diet

igh = /ī/

high	flight	frighten
light	night	tonight
fight	might	highway
bright	sight	
right	tight	

i-e = /ī/

nine	time	drive	alike	decide
wife	like	knife	alive	describe
fire	life	quite	inside	divide
mine	fine	twice	surprise	subscribe
mile	wide	while	entire	require

ie = /ī/

pie	tie
die	lie
cried	

y = /ī/

my	by	cypress	supply	tyrant
fly	dry	cyclone	nearby	occupy
sky	why	cycle	deny	hypothesis
try	buy	dynamite	rely	identify
cry	guy	hydrant	reply	modify

o = /ō/

no	ago	moment	radio	emotion
so	open	local	November	poetry
go	over	broken	appropriate	explosion
	also	motion	association	ferocious
	hotel	ocean	diploma	location

closed o = /ō/

gold	colt	roll	clothing	hostess
old	bolt	toll	enroll	patrol
told	both	poll	enfold	postage
hold	comb	most	behold	bolster
fold	ghost	post	golden	upholster

o-e = /ō/

rose	tone	drove	alone	telephone
vote	note	spoke	suppose	envelope
rope	sole	those	oppose	antelope
nose	rode	whole	remote	microscope
home	hole	wrote	postpone	artichoke

oa = /ō/

oak	soap	coach	toaster
oat	roast	coast	roadway
coat	loaf	throat	carload
boat	moan	boast	afloat
road	soak	float	approach

ow = /ō/

own	show	below	arrow
bowl	grow	follow	sorrow
know	snow	yellow	shadow
row	slow	narrow	tomorrow
low	flow	window	marshmallow

u = /ū/

unit	future	cucumber
united	human	distribution
uniform	music	university
usual	bugle	confusion
menu	humor	annual

u-e = /ū/

fuse	argue	amuse	distribute
cube	continue	perfume	pursue
mule	barbecue	refuse	statue
cue	rescue	accuse	virtue
huge	value	excuse	latitude

Other Vowels

al = /aw/

ball	salt	almost
call	walk	also
fall	talk	always
tall	false	although
wall	small	already

au = /aw/

fault	applause	cause	daughter
haul	audience	caught	exhausted
taught	August		

aw = /aw/

saw	paw	awful	law	straw
awkward	claw	hawk	strawberry	draw
crawl	withdraw	jaw	yawn	drawbridge

o = /aw/

off	long	across
on	strong	along
dog	wrong	often
cost	soft	belong
cross	loss	coffee

oi = /oy/

oil	point	appoint
join	coin	avoid
soil	moist	moisture
voice	boil	poison
noise	coin	disappoint

oy = /oy/

boy	enjoy	toy
annoy	joy	destroy
voyage	loyal	

ou = /ow/

out	south	about	announce
house	sound	amount	pronounce
hour	round	account	compound
loud	mouth	mountain	fountain
doubt	shout	thousand	roundabout

ow = /ow/

cow	brown	flower
now	clown	power
how	owl	vowel
down	growl	allow
crown	howl	shower

ew = /o͞o/

flew	new
crew	blew
chew	threw
drew	jewel
grew	jewelry

o, o-e = /o͞o/

to	prove	who
move	do	whose
two	remove	movement

oo = /o͞o/

moon	boot	school	balloon	noodle
food	cool	smooth	cartoon	shampoo
soon	fool	choose	cocoon	kangaroo
tool	noon	broom	racoon	igloo
too	room	shoot	gloomy	toothache

ou = /o͞o/

you	coupon
group	cougar
soup	routine
youth	through
wound	route

u = /o͞o/

truth	solution
student	revolution
duty	opportunity
junior	conclusion
tuba	constitution

u-e = /o͞o/

due	rude	pollute	barbecue
sue	tune	reduce	introduce
rule	dune	produce	attitude
June	flute	salute	gratitude
tube	brute	include	institute

oo, ou = /o͝o/

book	hook	could
foot	shook	should
look	stood	would
good	brook	
took	crook	

u = /o͝o/

bull	sugar
full	bully
pull	pudding
push	bullet
bush	plural

R Vowels

ar = /ar/

car	yard	charge	argue	depart
art	dark	start	artist	market
arm	bark	sharp	carpet	pardon
star	barn	card	garden	target
park	barn	guard	garbage	alarm

are = /air/

care	square	aware	hare
spare	beware	rare	stare
compare	scare	flare	warehouse
share	glare	welfare	

air = /air/

chair	fair
hair	dairy
pair	upstairs
flair	repair
stairs	millionaire

ear = /air/

bear	pear
tear	wear

ear = /ər/

earn	earl
early	pearl
earth	heard
learn	research
search	rehearse

er = /ər/

her	were	certain	nervous	determine
germ	nerve	expert	observe	emergency
herd	merge	hermit	permit	external
jerk	verb	perfect	prefer	internal
serve	swerve	person	serpent	permanent

ir = /ər/

bird	chirp	stir	squirrel
girl	first	thirst	virtue
dirt	shirt	whirl	thirteen
fir	firm	squirt	circle
sir	skirt	squirm	thirty

or, our = /ər/

word	worthy	courage	work
worse	courtesy	worry	worst
journey	worm	world	journal
worth	thorough	nourish	

ur = /ər/

burn	curtain	occur	furniture
church	furnace	purchase	suburban
curb	further	purple	burdensome
burst	hurry	purpose	occurrence
curl	murder	return	disturbance

or, our = /or/

or	port	pork	horses	ordinary	your
for	short	north	former	important	four
corn	form	porch	formed	organization	court
born	storm	score	order	performance	detour
torn	fort	sports	northern	adorable	tournament

ear, eer = /ear/

ear	clear	deer	dear
appear	cheer	hear	spearmint
steer	year	dreary	reindeer
fear	weary	volunteer	

Schwa

a = /ə/

above	alone	paragraph
around	allow	realize
about	agree	machine
another	afford	Pacific
ago	America	material

e = /ə/

camel	towel	amazement	open	avenue
happen	waken	apartment	silent	boulevard
jewel	oven	necessary	student	comedy
level	flannel	appointment	broken	courtesy
nickel	quarrel	judgment	parent	envelope

i = /ə/

visit	divide	ability	charity	evidence
limit	animal	application	confident	hesitant
unit	officer	principal	similar	identify
evil	difficult	accident	editor	original
direct	giraffe	cavity	multiply	criminal

o = /ə/

observe	opinion	atom	decision
obtain	official	economy	condition
other	original	revolution	division
concern	connection	democratic	develop
complete	protect	opposite	period

u = /ə/

suppose	circus
supply	focus
success	minus
bonus	asparagus
chorus	instrument

CHAPTER V

PHONOGRAMS

PHONOGRAMS, word families, or graphemic bases, as they are sometimes called, have been an important element in phonics instruction since at least the early 1880s (Smith, 1965). Previously, a phonogram was defined as almost any combination of consonant(s) and vowel that formed a syllable but not a whole word. Today phonograms are more carefully delineated and generally include consonant-ending combinations of a vowel and consonant(s) that can be used, with the addition of an initial consonant or consonant combination, to form a word.

Teaching phonics through phonograms is an effective technique according to research by Neuman (1981). This technique is also fast and efficient. For example, by adding initial consonants to the phonogram -at, students may learn how to decode a number of words: at, cat, fat, hat, Nat, pat, rat, and sat. The word vat could also be presented. However, this word does not occur frequently and would be unknown to many youngsters. When presenting phonograms or other phonic elements, it is important to balance ease of decoding with the utility of the words and the probability that the words will be part of the students' listening/speaking vocabulary.

PRESENTING PHONOGRAMS

Phonograms are often presented in a list of whole words. For example, the teacher might write the following -at words on the board, read them and/or have the students read them, and have them used in oral sentences. The teacher would note that all the words end in at and might also point out that each word begins with a different consonant.

81

cat	fat	hat	sat	rat

A more active way to present phonograms would be to present the phonogram and have students use initial consonants to build words. For example, the teacher might write -at on the board and have students tell what letter would be added to make the word **hat**. Four or five other words could then be formed in the same way (**bat, fat, mat, sat**). These would be written in a column on the board. The teacher would discuss how the words are the same (end in **at**) and how they are different (begin with a different letter). After discussing the complete list, students would supply other words that fit the pattern (**Nat, pat, rat**). The need to form real words would be stressed. If students suggest a nonsense word (**dat**), they would be asked if they had ever heard that word or if that is a real word. By using a building procedure, students learn a new phonogram and also review initial consonants.

MAJOR PHONOGRAMS

Included in this section are lists of major phonograms. Short vowel phonograms are listed first, followed by long vowel phonograms, other vowel phonograms, and r vowel phonograms. Like other phonic elements, phonograms also have their exceptions. The **at** in **what** does not have the same pronunciation as in **hat** and **cat**. The **and** in **wand** differs from the **and** in **band** and **hand**. There is also a degree of dialect variation. The phonogram **-en** as in **hen, ten, when** has a short **i** pronunciation in some regions. The **og** phonogram as in **dog** and **log** has a short **o** pronunciation in some areas and an /aw/ as in **law** pronunciation in others.

Short Vowel Phonograms

Short a

-ack	-ad	-ag	-am	-amp	-an
back	bad	bag	bam	camp	can
jack	dad	gag	dam	damp	Dan
pack	had	hag	ham	lamp	fan
sack	lad	rag	jam	ramp	man
tack	mad	tag	Pam	champ	Nan
shack	pad	brag	wham	stamp	pan
black	sad	drag	slam		tan
stack			scram		than
			swam		plan

-and	-ang	-ank	-ap	-at
and	bang	bank	cap	bat
band	fang	sank	gap	cat
hand	gang	tank	lap	fat
land	hang	yank	map	hat
sand	rang	blank	rap	Nat
brand	sang	crank	tap	pat
grand	Tang	drank	wrap	rat
stand	clang	spank	chap	sat
			clap	brat
			flap	chat
			slap	flat
			snap	
			trap	

Short e

-ed	-ell	-en	-end	-ent	-est	-et
bed	bell	Ben	bend	bent	best	bet
fed	dell	den	lend	dent	guest	get
red	fell	hen	mend	rent	nest	jet
Ted	Nell	Ken	send	sent	pest	let
wed	tell	men	tend	tent	rest	met
shed	well	pen	blend	went	test	net
bled	yell	when	spend	spent	west	pet
Fred	shell				chest	set
sled	smell					wet
sped						

Short i

-id	-ig	-ill	-im	-in
bid	big	bill	dim	bin
did	dig	dill	him	fin
hid	fig	fill	Jim	pin
kid	pig	gill	Kim	sin
lid	rig	hill	rim	tin
rid	wig	Jill	Tim	win
Sid	twig	kill	skim	chin
grid		mill	slim	thin
skid		pill	swim	grin
slid		sill		skin
		will		spin
		chill		twin
		drill		
		skill		
		spill		

-ing	-ink	-ip	-it
king	link	dip	bit
ring	mink	lip	fit
sing	pink	rip	hit
wing	rink	sip	kit
thing	sink	tip	knit
bring	wink	zip	pit
sling	think	chip	sit
sting	blink	ship	quit
	clink	whip	split
	drink	flip	
	stink	quip	
		skip	
		slip	
		trip	

Short o

-ob	-ock	-og	-op	-ot
Bob	dock	bog	cop	cot
cob	knock	fog	hop	dot
job	lock	jog	mop	got
knob	mock	hog	pop	hot
mob	rock	log	top	lot
rob	sock	clog	chop	not
sob	shock	frog	shop	pot
snob	block	smog	drop	rot
	clock		flop	shot
	flock		slop	blot
	stock		stop	clot
				slot
				trot
				spot

Short u

-ub	-uck	-uff	-ug	-um
cub	duck	buff	bug	bum
rub	luck	cuff	dug	hum
sub	puck	huff	hug	sum
tub	suck	puff	jug	yum
club	tuck	bluff	rug	chum
scrub	chuck	fluff	tug	drum
stub	cluck	scuff	chug	glum
	stuck	stuff	snug	plum
	truck			

-ump	-un	-ung	-unk	-ut
bump	bun	hung	bunk	but
dump	fun	rung	dunk	cut
hump	gun	sung	hunk	hut
jump	run	flung	junk	nut
lump	sun	slung	punk	rut
pump	shun	stung	sunk	shut
thump			chunk	
plump			skunk	
slump			spunk	
stump			stunk	

Long Vowel Phonograms

Long a

-ace	-ade	-ake		-ale	-ame	-ane
face	fade	bake	take	gale	came	cane
lace	jade	cake	wake	dale	fame	lane
mace	made	fake	shake	male	game	mane
pace	blade	Jake	flake	pale	lame	sane
race	grade	lake	brake	sale	name	crane
brace	shade	make	snake	tale	same	
grace	spade	rake	stake	scale	tame	
place	trade	sake		stale	shame	
space					blame	
trace						

-ate	-ave	-aid	-ail	-ain	-ay
date	cave	aid	bail	main	bay
fate	gave	laid	fail	pain	day
gate	pave	maid	hail	rain	hay
hate	rave	paid	jail	chain	lay
late	save	raid	mail	brain	may
mate	wave	braid	nail	drain	pay
Nate	shave		pail	grain	ray
rate	brave		rail	train	say
plate	grave		sail	stain	way
slate	slave		tail		gray
skate			wail		play
state			trail		slay
			snail		tray

Long e

-eak	-eal	-eam	-eat	-eed	-eep	-eet
beak	deal	beam	beat	deed	beep	beet
leak	heal	team	neat	feed	deep	feet
peak	meal	dream	seat	heed	jeep	meet
teak	Neal	gleam	cheat	reed	keep	sheet
weak	real	scream	wheat	seed	peep	fleet
creak	seal	steam	bleat	weed	weep	sleet
freak	veal		treat	bleed	cheep	sweet
sneak	squeal			freed	sheep	
speak	steal			speed	creep	
squeak					sleep	
					steep	

Long i

-ice	-ide	-ime	-ine	-ive	-ind	-y
dice	bide	dime	dine	dive	bind	by
lice	hide	lime	fine	five	find	guy
mice	ride	time	line	hive	kind	my
nice	side	chime	mine	jive	mind	why
rice	tide	slime	nine	live	rind	shy
slice	wide		pine	chive	wind	dry
spice	bride		vine	drive	blind	fly
twice	slide		wine			sky
			thine			sly
						try

Long o

-oke	-one	-ope	-ow	-old
joke	bone	dope	bow	hold
poke	cone	hope	low	cold
woke	tone	mope	mow	fold
choke	phone	nope	tow	gold
broke	shone	rope	show	hold
smoke	throne	slope	blow	mold
spoke			glow	sold
			slow	told
			snow	

Other Vowel Phonograms

/aw/

-al	-aw	-ought
ball	caw	bought
call	jaw	fought
fall	law	nought
hall	paw	sought
mall	raw	thought
tall	saw	brought
wall	claw	
small	draw	
stall	flaw	
	slaw	
	straw	

/oi/

-oi	-oy
oil	boy
boil	coy
coil	joy
foil	soy
soil	toy
toil	

Short oo

-ook

book	cook
hook	look
took	shook
brook	crook

Long oo

-oot

boot	loot
moot	root
toot	shoot
scoot	

/ow/

-ou	-ow
out	bow
bout	cow
pout	how
shout	now
scout	pow
spout	sow
stout	wow
	chow
	plow

R Vowel Phonograms

/air/

-air	-are		-ear
fair	bare	blare	bear
hair	care	Clare	pear
pair	fare	flare	tear
chair	hare	glare	swear
	mare	scare	
	rare	spare	
	ware	square	
	share		

/ar/

-ar	-ark	-art
bar	ark	art
car	bark	Bart
far	dark	dart
jar	hark	mart
par	lark	part
tar	mark	chart
char	park	smart
scar	shark	
star	spark	

/ear/

-ear	-eer
dear	beer
fear	deer
gear	jeer
hear	peer
near	seer
rear	cheer
year	sheer
shear	queer
clear	sneer
smear	steer
spear	

/or/

-ore	-orn
bore	born
core	corn
fore	torn
lore	worn
more	scorn
sore	sworn
tore	
wore	
chore	
shore	
score	
store	
swore	

CHAPTER VI

DECODING MULTISYLLABIC WORDS

LARGE NUMBERS of students master single-syllable phonics but have difficulty applying their knowledge of sound-symbol relationships to multisyllabic words. Part of the blame may lie in the way syllabication is taught. First of all, there is some confusion about the purpose of syllabication. For reading, all the student needs to do is to break the words into smaller units that can be handled more readily than the whole word. It isn't necessary for the student to split words exactly as they might be divided for end-of-line hyphenation. The student then pronounces each part, puts the parts together, and pronounces the whole word. As long as the student is able to reconstruct the word, it doesn't matter what kinds of units are used. Insisting upon precise word division is a legitimate demand for dividing words when writing or typing but not for reading.

Another point of confusion has to do with visual versus auditory syllabication. Words are divided into two kinds of syllables in the dictionary: orthographic and phonemic. Orthographic syllables are meant for end-of-line divisions (**rev o lu tion ary**). Phonemic syllables represent divisions in a word according to the way it's pronounced (**rev o lu tio nar y**). Often the two are the same, but they may vary. For example, in the following words, orthographic and phonemic syllabication don't match.

Orthographic	Phonemic
ap ply	a pply
at ten tion	a tten tion
emer gen cy	e mer gen cy
gen er ous	gen (e) rous

Orthographic syllabication is important in writing. Phonemic syllabication is important in reading. When the two differ, phonemic rather than orthographic syllabication should be used when trying to sound out a multisyllabic word.

ATTACKING MULTISYLLABIC WORDS

Here is what students should do when faced with a multisyllabic word which they are unable to pronounce.

Step 1: Break the word down into its approximate syllables. If the word has affixes, students should start with the prefix, go to the suffix, and then go to the root word. Otherwise students should start with the first syllable and work from left to right. Occasionally, students might spot a pronounceable unit in the middle or end of the word and go from right to left. As Durkin (1981) noted, syllabication is a pragmatic process. Whatever works is acceptable.

Syllabication need not be an exact process. As Harris and Sipay (1985) explain, a student could analyze the word treaty as **treat-y, tr-ea-ty,** or **trea-ty** and still pronounce the word accurately.

Step 2: Pronounce each syllable as accurately as possible. Often, however, one syllable in a word will be the key that helps students pronounce the rest of the word.

Step 3: Put the syllables together to form a whole word.

Step 4: If the resulting product is not a real word, adjust the pronunciation of one or more syllables until a real word is pronounced.

Step 5: The reconstructed word should be checked in context.

SYLLABICATION GENERALIZATIONS

To aid in the process of dividing words into syllables syllabication generalizations are taught in most reading programs. The most useful generalizations include those described below.

Compound Words

The separate words in a compound word usually form separate syllables: **day light, base ball.**

This generalization helps students because breaking the compound into its components makes it easier to pronounce the whole word, and the components often suggest the meaning of the whole word: **sunset, popcorn.** However, this is not always so. The words **break** and **fast** change their pronunciation when they are joined into a compound. While the individual words **break** and **fast** might give clues to the whole word, the clues would be too sophisticated for most youngsters.

Affixes

Prefixes and suffixes often form separate syllables: **hope less, pre view.**

This is a highly useful generalization because a large percentage of words contain affixes. Occasionally, spellings are changed when affixes are added as in **happiness, hopped.** Less frequently, pronunciations of the base words are altered when affixes are added: **medicinal, partial.** There are also some rare instances when an affix draws on a sound from the base word when forming a syllable: **pamphleteer** /pam flih TEER/, **profiteer** /prof ih TEER/.

Two Consonants Between Two Vowels

When two consonants come together between two vowels, they are usually divided between the two consonants: **shel ter.** Often there is a corollary that says digraphs are not divided: **moth er.**

This generalization is useful because it helps the student break words into pronounceable units. It can also be an indication of the pronunciation of the first vowel. A vowel in a syllable that ends in a consonant is often short. Thus, the first syllable in **ladder** is short, but the first syllable in **labor** is long.

Single Consonant Between Two Vowels

A single consonant between two vowels usually goes with the second vowel: **lo cal, ba con.**

This generalization is useful because it applies with a fair degree of consistency to a significant number of words. Along with the generalization, students are taught that open syllables usually have a long vowel. Since this generalization has a fair number of exceptions (**wag on, sev en**), students need to be taught to be flexible. If the long vowel pronunciation doesn't work out, students should try the short vowel pronunciation. Context, of course, should also be used.

GENERALIZATIONS THAT HAVE LIMITED APPLICATION

Some syllabication rules that are frequently taught have limited utility. These include generalizations similar to the following.

Final le

Final **le** usually combines with the preceding consonant to form a separate syllable: **pur ple, ta ble.** This generalization assists somewhat with the pronunciation of **table** because it helps the student see that the first syllable is open and so the vowel would be long. The generalization doesn't help much with a word like **purple** because even if the reader divided between **p** and **le,** he or she should still end up with the right pronunciation.

Ed When Preceded by T or D

Ed when preceded by **t** or **d** forms a separate syllable: **plan ted, mol ded.** It is difficult to see how this generalization would help students with their decoding.

TEACHING SYLLABICATION

In some reading programs, syllabication is introduced in first grade. In most programs, syllabication isn't presented until grade three. However, an examination of words used in grade two basals according to the Harris-Jacobson list (1982) indicate that approximately 38 percent of them are multisyllabic.

If presented carefully, syllabication skills can be taught before grade three. Here is how the concept of syllabication might be introduced.

Auditory Perception of Word Parts

Before students can divide words into syllables, they must be able to hear the syllables in a word. Tell students that words have parts that you can hear. Point out that some words have one part, but others have two parts or even more. Tell students to listen as you say some words. Explain that you will clap for each word part. Say the following words. Emphasize the separate syllables and clap as you say each one: **sunup, sunset, sundown, daylight, morning, because, window, grandma,** anything, apple, picture, outside, become, bedtime, Monday, Tuesday, neighbor.

Once students have caught on to the idea, say the following words and have them clap along: **Tuesday, empty, farmer, finish, homework, moonlight, certain, daytime, cookie, lunchroom, lonely, meow, nobody, giant, forgot, forest.**

As students become proficient, supply them with three-syllable words: **grandmother, happily, important, wonderful, scientist, adventure.**

Say your last name and have students say how many word parts it has. Then have each student carefully pronounce his or her last name and have the rest of the class tell how many syllables are in the name.

Visual Perception of Syllables

Have students demonstrate chants that they use while jumping rope. Point out that these chants are said syllable by syllable. Write some of these chants on the chalkboard in syllables. Read the chant, pointing to each syllable as you do so (from an idea suggested by Edward Fry).

Give students copies of sheet music of easy songs. Have the class sing the songs. Point out that the words are divided into syllables so that the singer can give the song the right beat. Examine some of the words that have been written in syllables. Say the words, emphasizing the syllables. Discuss the fact that in each syllable a vowel sound can be heard and a vowel letter or pair of letters can be seen. Lead students to see that a word generally has as many syllables as it has sounded vowels. (Technically, word-final l and n often function as syllabic consonants or syllables: **rattle**, /RATəl/, **mitten**, /MITən/.)

Presentation of Pattern Generalization

Present a syllable pattern and/or generalization that would be useful at this point. For example, if students are about to read a selection that contains a number of compound words, introduce the compound word generalization. Use a single-syllable to provide a contrast. For example, place the following on the chalkboard:

sun	ball
sunup	football
sunset	baseball
sundown	handball

Have students read the word **sun** and the words underneath **sun.** Have students notice that **sun** is a part of the words underneath it. Follow a similar procedure with **ball** and the words underneath it.

Practice

• Have students fill in sentence blanks with compound words and compose compound words by joining parts of single-syllable words.

• Compose an experience story in which compound words are likely to be used: story about baseball or a sunset or footprints.

Application

Have students read a story that contains compound words. If necessary, help them divide the words into syllables. Encourage students to use syllabication as a tool to help them attack multisyllabic words in any reading that they do.

REINFORCEMENT ACTIVITIES

• Have students match syllables to create words. The exercise should illustrate a particular pattern or generalization. The following exercise centers around the long **a,** open syllable pattern.

1. la	a. per
2. pa	b. bor
3. ma	c. dar
4. ra	d. ple

• Have students put scrambled syllables together to form words. This kind of activity focuses on pronounceable word parts and emphasizes that words recreated by putting syllables together should be meaningful. Words used should be limited to those that are already in students' listening/speaking vocabularies.

u	ed	ca	tion	
ca	tion	lo		
lu	pol	tion		
er	res	tion	va	
ab	i	tion	brev	a

• Have students complete sentences by choosing from contrasting words. This leads students to use context and notice internal syllables.

A blip showed up on the (ray, radar, radio) screen.

Not sure where he was, the lost pilot could not give his (low, locate, location).

The (pie, piper, pilot) landed the jet.

• Use song lyrics to give students practice in attacking multisyllabic words. Supply students with copies of lyrics from songs appropriate to their level of development. Have the class sing the lyrics, paying particular attention to multisyllabic words. Use the following or other easy-to-understand traditional or popular songs:

"I've Been Working on the Railroad"
"Toyland"
"Clementine"
"Home on the Range"
"Red River Valley"
"Oh! Susanna"
"The Erie Canal"
"Wait for the Wagon"
"Hush Little Baby"

PATTERNS

Along with useful syllabication generalizations, students should be taught frequently occurring patterns of syllabication. Students may have trouble applying generalizations. However, presentation of syllabication patterns helps them perceive and automatically use frequently occurring pronounceable elements that appear in multisyllabic words. High frequency syllable patterns arranged in approximate order of difficulty are listed below.

Compound Words

sunup	birthday
sundown	grandma
outside	grandpa
inside	anybody
maybe	anyone
anything	himself
something	herself
someday	baseball
sometime	football

-ing Words

fishing	making	running
helping	riding	batting
jumping	hiding	cutting
playing	saying	sitting
reading	taking	swimming
calling	liking	hitting
falling	naming	planning
feeling	biting	shopping
finding	facing	fitting
growing	racing	flipping

-ly Words

friendly	happily
quickly	sleepily
slowly	angrily
kindly	noisily
meanly	prettily
mostly	easily
nearly	heavily

Easy Prefixes

unhappy	reread
unknown	refill
unpack	retell
unhurt	repaint
unafraid	rewrite

Easy Suffixes

careless	careful	farmer
helpless	helpful	helper
needless	hopeful	player
sleepless	thankful	baker
colorless	hurtful	planter

Schwa a Words

ago	ahead
alone	apart
along	asleep
again	agree
another	abound
around	account
about	adult
across	alive
afraid	allow
among	aloud

Closed Syllable, Short a Words

napkin	batter	candle
basket	passer	handle
rabbit	chapter	gamble
magnet	charter	paddle
plastic	clatter	saddle
tablet	manner	sample
planet	hamster	tackle
canvas	platter	tangle
cancel	matter	spangle
captain	trapper	trample

Closed Syllable, Short e Words

letter	hello	temple
better	fellow	kennel
center	sentence	pebble
pepper	sensible	settle
temper	lettuce	tentacle
tender	tennis	helmet
cellar	lesson	dessert
shelter	velvet	trespass
pester	pennant	splendid
western	seldom	welfare

Closed Syllable, Short i Words

dizzy	bitter	little	mitten
skinny	clipper	middle	kitten
victim	dinner	pickle	ribbon
village	glitter	nimble	children
willow	hinder	quibble	listen
witness	swimmer	simple	glisten
blizzard	winner	dimple	cinnamon
chimney	whisper	twinkle	million
distant	simmer	crinkle	billion
district	cinder	dribble	fiction

e = /i/ Words

enjoy	began	remain
entire	became	regard
enough	between	remember
effect	beneath	respect
event	behind	reply
electric	decide	require
election	describe	relation
express	defense	receive
except	demand	reception
explain	degree	refrigerator

age = /ij/ Words

baggage	percentage
cabbage	postage
garbage	sausage
bandage	courage
village	savage
manage	hostage
damage	advantage
leakage	wreckage
message	voyage

Closed Syllable, Short o Words

rocket	follow	doctor	bottle
problem	gossip	bother	gobble
bottom	hockey	copper	nozzle
contest	lobster	dollar	topple
common	cottage	holler	throttle
comment	broccoli	robber	wobble
congress	costume	shopper	
context	contrast	sponsor	
cotton	conference	totter	

Closed Syllable, Short u Words

button	number	jungle
hundred	summer	buckle
husband	drummer	bubble
pumpkin	runner	mumble
punish	rubber	fumble
subject	hunger	grumble
sudden	thunder	huddle
luggage	lumber	humble
muffin	muffler	hustle
mustard	mutter	jumble

Open Syllable, Long a Words

baby	paper	able
basic	labor	table
bacon	favor	fable
acorn	flavor	label
agent	gravy	cable
radio	navy	stable
lady	native	maple
lazy	patience	nation
nature	vacant	station
hazy	famous	location

Digraph ai/ay Words

afraid	dismay
remain	display
complain	payment
contain	portray
detail	mayonnaise

E Marker, Long a Words

awake	persuade
arrange	donate
engage	separate
enrage	advocate
escape	amputate
humane	dislocate
replace	abbreviate
donate	appreciate
calculate	associate
female	exaggerate

Open Syllable, Long e Words

even	recent
evil	reappear
equal	detour
zebra	legal
female	premium
fever	regal
secret	region
cedar	meter
tepee	meteor
vehicle	ingredient

E Marker, Long e Words

complete	concrete
extreme	precede
supreme	stampede
trapeze	centipede

Digraph ee, Long e Words

agree	discreet
asleep	proceed
between	succeed
freedom	degree
canteen	guarantee

Digraph ea, Long e Words

reason	measles
repeat	conceal
deceased	impeach
ordeal	eagle
beagle	

Open Syllable, Long i Words

tiny	tiger
lilac	spider
digest	diver
climate	minor
ivy	miser
pirate	rifle
sinus	bicycle
vinyl	bridle
vital	final

E Marker, Long i Words

alike	surprise
alive	revise
aside	subscribe
beside	prescribe
decide	survive
divide	advise
provide	collide
despite	confide
invite	confine
recite	refine

Final y, Long i Words

modify	terrify
satisfy	testify
occupy	notify
identify	beautify
dignify	classify

Open Syllable, Long o Words

noble	local	notice
vocal	hotel	quota
motel	soda	echo
locust	hero	robot
okay	rodent	open
rotate	over	token
ocean	total	oval
soda	broker	cozy
chosen	cocoa	

E Marker, Long o Words

alone	arose
awoke	compose
corrode	remote
demote	disclose
enclose	explode

Open Syllable, Long u Words

bugle	humor
music	humid
future	puny
pupil	cucumber
human	unit

E Marker, Long u Words

amuse	continue
accuse	rescue
excuse	value
confuse	issue
commute	tissue

au/aw = /aw/ Words

author	awful
autumn	awkward
audience	strawberry
August	
auditorium	
autograph	
caution	
cautious	
faucet	
saucer	

oi/oy = /oi/ Words

annoy	appoint
destroy	avoid
loyal	moisten
employ	moisture
employee	rejoice
enjoy	ointment
voyage	poison

ou/ow = /ow/ Words

aloud	allow
around	coward
announce	drowsy
account	flower
counter	power
council	powder
county	shower
fountain	towel
mountain	tower
pronounce	vowel

Open Syllable, u = /o͞o/ Words

tuna	stupid	junior
ruby	student	nuclear
rumor	super	revolution
rhubarb	duty	institution
truant	tuba	opportunity
brutal	tulip	inclusion

oo = /o͞o/ Words

balloon	raccoon
bamboo	kangaroo
baboon	doodle
shampoo	noodle
tattoo	cuckoo
cartoon	igloo

oo = /o͝o/ Words

afoot	booklet
understood	woolen
wooden	handbook
neighborhood	

ar, are, air = /air/ Words

aware	affair
beware	despair
compare	prairie
declare	repair
prepare	millionaire
parent	billionaire
vary	questionnaire
canary	transparent
library	malaria

ar = /ar/ Words

barber	alarm
bargain	apart
cargo	depart
carton	discard
cartoon	compartment
farmer	regard
garbage	remark
garden	partner
garment	pharmacy
target	boulevard

er, ear, ere, eer = /ear/ Words

hero	appear
zero	weary
period	spearmint
serious	severe
cereal	sincere
superior	atmosphere
material	pioneer
mysterious	volunteer
cafeteria	career
experience	engineer

er = /ər/ Words

perfect	alert
nervous	concern
person	transfer
permit	adverb
perfume	reverse
servant	expert
merchant	observe
certain	emergency
jersey	terminal
kernel	thermostat

ur = /ər/ Words

turkey	burden
turnip	burglar
turtle	burrow
return	hurdle
curtain	hurricane
current	murder
purple	murmur
purchase	turmoil
furnace	survey
furniture	survive

ir, or, our = /ər/ Words

circle	actor	janitor
circus	author	motor
sirloin	anchor	odor
squirrel	doctor	major
thirsty	editor	janitor
courage	favor	radiator
journey	flavor	rumor
nourish	elevator	senior
courtesy	governor	tractor
		attorney
		worthless

or = /or/ Words

forty	former
forward	formula
fortune	fortunate
border	perform
corner	reform
order	uniform
orbit	distort
orchard	enormous
orchestra	shorten
morning	shortage

ti = /sh/ Words

action	addition	circulation
caution	attention	definition
mention	affection	exclamation
fiction	collection	graduation
fraction	connection	hesitation
lotion	construction	imagination
junction	convention	occupation
motion	correction	population
nation	description	reputation
portion	direction	revolution

y = /ē/ Words

baby	candy	family
lady	penny	party
tiny	fifty	worry
icy	city	bakery
pony	puppy	bravery
navy	hungry	canary
shady	happy	celery
easy	fully	colony
needy	ready	company
sleepy	heavy	enemy

t = /ch/ Words

nature	pasture
future	fortune
picture	adventure
capture	fracture
feature	signature
creature	temperature
posture	actual
torture	natural
statue	century

el, al, ol = /əl/ Words

camel	cancel
jewel	angel
level	gospel
model	mental
nickel	rascal
towel	sandal
pedal	signal
plural	symbol
royal	vocal
loyal	local

le = /əl/ Words

apple	title
cattle	Bible
little	table
middle	cable
bottle	fable
bubble	stable
buckle	beetle
castle	eagle
chuckle	needle
drizzle	noble

Adjacent Sounded Vowel Words

giant	radio
diet	radiator
quiet	audio
liar	area
riot	stereo
trial	video
triangle	fluid
poem	ruin
poet	duel
create	cruel

CHAPTER VII

TEACHING OTHER WORD ATTACK SKILLS

PHONICS and syllabication should not be used to the exclusion of other word attack skills. Sight vocabulary, knowledge of contractions, morphemic analysis, context clues, and dictionary skills are also essential word attack skills. The best decoding program is one that uses all of these skills in an integrated approach.

SIGHT VOCABULARY

Some words have such irregular spellings that memorizing them is the best way to learn them. **Of, one** and, to a lesser extent, **does** and **have** are good examples of words that are best memorized or learned as sight words.

Some words are highly regular and so could be presented through a phonics approach but embody letter-sound relationships that may not be taught until fairly late in some programs. If these words have a high frequency and/or are needed to craft primer selections, they might be introduced as sight words. Such words might include **green, be,** and **show.**

Some words, such as **the, a, of, at,** and **it,** occur with such high frequency that it would be difficult to read a paragraph or sentence that doesn't contain some of them. To help students gain fluency in their reading, it is a good idea to present high frequency words of this type in such a way that students learn to recognize them immediately and so don't have to sound them out. Excessive sounding out causes students to lose the gist of what they are reading and hinders comprehension. It also makes it more difficult for them to use context clues. Even though high frequency words like **at** and **it** are easily decoded, students should learn to read these words at sight so they won't get bogged down sounding them out.

There are a number of lists of high frequency words that students should recognize instantly, or at sight, but the Dolch (1936), the oldest of these lists, is still the most popular. The Dolch list is comprised of 220 words drawn primarily from words frequently spoken by kindergarten children and which also appeared in children's reading materials. These 220 words make up more than 60 percent of the words in running text contained in a primary basal.

A list of Dolch words is contained in Table XIII. All but eighteen of the Dolch words appear on the first-grade level of the Harris-Jacobson list (1982). Those eighteen words can be found on the second-grade level of the Harris-Jacobson list and are starred in Table XIII.

TABLE XIII
Dolch List of 220 Sight Words

a	find	many	stop
about	first	may	take
after	five*	me	tell
again	fly	much	ten*
all	for	must	thank
always	found	my	that
am	four	myself	the
an	from	never	their
and	full*	new	them
any	funny	no	then
are	gave	not	there
around	get	now	these
as	give	of	they
ask	go	off	think
at	goes	old	this
ate	going	on	those
away	good	once*	three
be	got	one	to
because	green	only	today
been	grow	open	together
before*	had	or	too
best	has	our	try
better	have	out	two
big	he	over	under
black	help	own*	up
blue	her	pick	upon*
both*	here	play	us

Table XIII (*continued*)

bring*	him	please	use
brown	his	pretty	very
but	hold	pull	walk
buy	hot	put	want
by	how	ran	warm*
call	hurt	read	was
came	I	red	wash*
can	if	ride	we
carry*	in	right	well
clean	into	round*	went
cold	is	run	were
come	it	said	what
could	its	saw	when
cut	jump	say	where
did	just	see	which
do	keep	seven*	white
does	kind	shall*	who
done*	know	she	why
don't	laugh	show	will
down	let	sing	wish
draw	light	sit	with
drink	like	six	work
eat	little	sleep	would
eight*	live	small	write*
every	long	so	yellow
fall	look	some	yes
far	made	soon	you
fast	make	start	your

In Table XIV, there is a list of 100 sight words especially prepared for older students. The words appeared among the most frequently occurring words on both the American Heritage list (Carroll, Davis, & Richman, 1971) and the Computational list (Kučera and Francis, 1967).

Although the Dolch list is well respected, the best list might be one compiled from the reading series your students are using. Lists of words are generally contained in the teacher's manuals. Choose from these lists words that are likely to occur early and frequently. Also choose high utility words whose spellings are irregular or rare.

In deciding which sight words to introduce first, consider ease of learning. In general nouns and special interest words and high imagery words are easiest to learn. For example, the word **fly** as a noun was

TABLE XIV

Sight Vocabulary for Older Students

1. the	26. from	51. up	76. now
2. of	27. or	52. so	77. my
3. and	28. not	53. him	78. how
4. a	29. have	54. them	79. may
5. to	30. but	55. more	80. new
6. in	31. one	56. been	81. made
7. is	32. an	57. do	82. over
8. that	33. all	58. into	83. did
9. he	34. which	59. some	84. after
10. it	35. there	60. then	85. way
11. was	36. we	61. no	86. down
12. for	37. were	62. who	87. most
13. with	38. when	63. other	88. make
14. on	39. their	64. these	89. see
15. as	40. said	65. its	90. our
16. his	41. what	66. than	91. man
17. at	42. she	67. two	92. any
18. are	43. will	68. time	93. where
19. I	44. if	69. your	94. through
20. be	45. would	70. could	95. people
21. you	46. can	71. many	96. me
22. this	47. her	72. like	97. back
23. by	48. out	73. first	98. before
24. they	49. about	74. only	99. little
25. had	50. has	75. each	100. just

more readily learned by kindergarteners than was the word **fly** as a verb. Distinctive shapes also apparently help young students learn words. The words **exercise** and **too** were readily learned by kindergarten pupils. Words that have both a high frequency and are easy to learn include: **yes, potatoes, rabbit, or, over, on, which, things, don't, car, me, snow, are, puppy, school, air, a, birthday, cookies, yellow, up, here, two, sun, street, pond,** and **night** (Sartain, 1981).

Teaching Sight Words

Should sight words be presented in context or isolation? The answer is both. Research by Samuels (1967) and Samuels and Spiroff (1973) suggests that presenting sight words in isolation forces students to focus on the letters that make up the word. However, context is important because many sight words are function words — prepositions, articles, and conjunctions — and need to be in context so that students can see how they are used. In addition, words presented in isolation are often given "list" stress. They are given a stress that doesn't usually occur in context. For example, the word **and** in isolation is pronounced /and/. In context, the vowel is not stressed and the final consonant might be dropped so that the word is pronounced /ən(d)/ as in: Bill and Bob are brothers. By hearing the word **and** spoken in context, students meet it the way it is usually spoken.

No more than four to seven sight words should be introduced at one time. The best words for introduction are those that will be immediately useful to students. Pick words that have a high frequency and which appear in an upcoming reading selection. Here are steps for introducing the sight word **like.**

Step 1: Developing Word in Listening/Speaking Vocabulary

Tell about some things that you like to do. Then have students tell about things they like to do.

Step 2: Presenting the Word in Written Context

On the chalkboard write: I like to ride my bike. Point to the word **like** as you read it. Underline the word **like.** Have other students read the sentence. (All the words in demonstration sentences, except the new sight word, should be words that students have previously learned to read.)

Step 3: Examining Distinguishing Characteristics

Ask students to look at the word **like** and spell it. Write **bike** under the word **like** and compare the two words. Compare **like** with other sight words that have been previously taught. For example, compare **like** with **look** and **little.**

Step 4: Practice

Have students keep a card file of sight words. Flash the sight words for about ten minutes each day so that students can respond to the words accurately and rapidly. When flashing the words, make sure that youngsters look at each word as they say it so that the association between the oral and written forms of each word is strengthened. Also have students create sentences using sight word cards and unscramble sentences composed of sight word cards (cake like I). See "Reinforcement Activities" below for additional practice ideas.

Step 5: Application

Have students read a story in their readers, a trade book, or an experience story that contains the word **like.**

Reinforcement Activities

• Have students read easy trade books. There is no better practice for fluency with sight words than sustained reading. See "Children's Books That Can Be Used to Reinforce Word Attack Skills" in Chapter XI for some suggested titles.

• Use commercially prepared computer programs or electronic devices for flashing words. Look for software that allows you to insert words of your own choosing. See Chapter XI for a listing of programs.

• Have students compose experience stories that reinforce recently taught sight words. For example, after introducing the sight word **like,** have students create "I Like" booklets. Each page will contain a drawing of something students like. It could be a favorite game, food, TV show, day, person, book, etc. Each drawing should have a caption telling what students like.

• Play concentration using sight words.

• Create board games that involve reading sight words. The spaces on the board's pathway would contain sight words. Students flick a spinner which points to a number from 1 to 5. They move their marker the number of spaces indicated and then read the sight word on the spot to which they have moved. If they can't read the word, they must move back to where they were. The winner is the person who reaches the ending spot first.

• Use signs and labels to reinforce sight words. For example, if you have one door for entering a room and another for exiting, place **In** and **Out** signs on the doors. Place **On** and **Off** signs on lights and other switches and **Up** and **Down** signs on elevator buttons.

• Have students place sight words in categories. Have them find number words, color words, words that tell size or how many.

• Have students pantomine action sight words: **sleep, run, eat, jump.**

• Have students respond to written commands: Walk; Read a book; Get a drink; Draw a pretty picture.

• Use a Language Master or other card reader. The cards for a card reader contain a strip of magnetic tape on which a brief message may be recorded. On one side of the card write the target sight word and tape the word so that students can see and hear the word. On the other side, write the word but do not record it. Instead, have students record their response as the card slides through the reader. Students may then check to see if their response is correct by putting the other side of the card through the card reader.

CONTRACTIONS

Although students use contractions in their everyday speech, they don't automatically recognize contractions in print. All students need to know in order to read contractions is that the printed contraction has the same function and meaning as its spoken form. They do not need to know, for example, that **can't** is a contraction composed of the words **can** plus **not** and that the missing **n-o** in **not** is signified by an apostrophe. This information is important for language arts but not for reading. Some youngsters may even be confused by the information and read the word **can't** as **can't not**.

Contractions can be taught in much the same way as sight words are presented. When learning the written form of the word **can't**, for example, students would discuss things that they **can't** do. The teacher would write a model sentence using **can't** and have the students read the sentence. The graphic characteristics of **can't** would be discussed. If she or he wishes, the teacher might explain the reason for the apostrophe, but this is not necessary. After practice activities with the word, students would read selections that contain the contraction **can't**.

Listed on the next page are frequently occurring contractions and the levels at which they first appear in most reading series.

MORPHEMIC ANALYSIS

As students grow in reading ability and meet longer, more complex words, morphemic analysis becomes a major decoding strategy. Phonics, syllabication, and letter clusters involve sound units. However, morphemic analysis consists of analyzing the meaning-bearing units of words. For example, the word **meaningful** has three meaning-bearing

TABLE XV

Frequently Occurring Contractions

First Grade	Second Grade	Third Grade
can't	hadn't	how's
don't	haven't	it'll
it's	he'd	mustn't
didn't	he'll	shouldn't
I'll	here's	they'd
I'm	I'd	they've
won't	she's	
you're	they'll	
doesn't	we'd	
he's	we're	
I've	weren't	
isn't	where's	
there's	who's	
wasn't	wouldn't	
we'll	you'd	
what's	you'll	
	you've	

units: **mean, ing,** and **ful.** Morphemic analysis deals with affixes (**pre-,
-less**) and root words (**port**) or combining forms (**graph**). (A combining
form is a word part that forms a word when another combining form
(**chron + ology**) or affix **chron + ic**) is added to it.)

Morphemic analysis is a highly promising word attack strategy. A
large percentage of the words in the English language contain affixes,
roots, or combining forms. Unfortunately, instruction in morphemic
analysis has been ineffective. According to research by Dale and
O'Rourke (1976), students make limited use of morphemic analysis. In
a longitudinal study of students' knowledge of reading vocabulary that
involved thousands of students, the researchers found that many youngsters did not have knowledge of prefixes and suffixes or could not apply
this knowledge. For example, the word **erase** is known by 76 percent of
fourth graders. The word **erasure** was familiar to only 72 percent of
eighth graders. The words **habit** and **elephant** were known by 69 percent and 89 percent of fourth graders. The words **habitual** and
elephantine were known by only 75 percent and 68 percent of tenth
graders.

Teaching Morphemic Units

As Deighton (1959) noted, there are three major limitations in using morphemic units to attack unfamiliar words. First of all, the units may have more than one meaning. For example, according to *Webster's Ninth New Collegiate Dictionary* (Mish, 1983), the prefix **co** has four main meanings: "with, in or to the same degree, one that is associated in action with another, and of or relating to" (p. 252).

In many words containing prefixes, the prefix is not obvious. The prefix has become such an integral part of the word that the reader is not aware of it. The word **deter**, for instance, is formed from the prefix **de** and the verb **terrere**, which means "to frighten from." Chances are, a reader having difficulty with this word would not realize that **de** is a prefix and that **ter** is formed from **terrere**.

A third limitation is that there are a number of words that look as though they have prefixes but don't. The words **irksome** and **iridescent**, for instance, do not contain the prefix **ir**.

Suffixes and, to a lesser extent, roots and combining forms, also suffer from the same limitations prefixes do. They often have several meanings or have been absorbed in words in such a way that they are no longer recognized.

Despite these limitations, morphemic elements provide the keys that help unlock many unfamiliar words. As Dale and O'Rourke (1971) have pointed out, morphemic elements can also be memory aids. They can help students remember new words.

Which morphemic elements should be taught? In general, the most frequently occurring and most useful units should be presented. Common prefixes and their meanings are listed in Table XVI. Common suffixes are listed in Table XVII.

TABLE XVI
Prefixes

Prefix	Meaning(s)	Example(s)
a-	not	atypical
ad-	to; toward	advance
anti-	against	antiwar
bi-	two; twice	bicycle
	coming every two	biweekly

Table XVI *(continued)*

Prefix	Meaning(s)	Example(s)
com-, co-, col-, con-, cor-	with; together	combination, co-worker collaborate connection correlate
counter-	opposite reacting to working with	counterclockwise counterattack counterbalance
de-	opposite taking from making less	decode dethrone devalue
dis-	not opposite	disloyal disconnect
en-, em-	in; into put into (makes verbs)	encase empower
ex-, e-	out; out of former	exhale, emit ex-quarterback
extra-	beyond	extracurricular
il-, im-, in-, ir-	not	illegal impossible independent irregular
in-	in; into	inhale
inter-	between; among	international
mis-	wrong; bad not; opposite	mislead misfortune
non-	not	nonflowing
para-	near; alongside related to but being under	parathyroid paramedic
per-	through; throughout	percolate
pre-	before	prepay
pro-	in favor of	prolabor
pro-	before	prologue
re-	again; back	reread, repay
semi-, sem-	half; partly	semicircle
sub-	under; below	subway
super-	over; above	supersonic
syn-	with	synchronize
trans-	across	transcontinental
un-	not	unafraid
uni-	one	unicycle
vice-	next in line; taking the place of	vice-president

TABLE XVII
Suffixes

Suffix	Meaning(s)	Example(s)
-able, -ible	can be	playable, possible
-ade	action	blockade
	product	lemonade
-age	action	breakage
	place	orphanage
-al	related to or	musical
	having action	rehearsal
-an, -ian	belong to or	Kentuckian
	coming from	
	working in the	beautician
	field of	
-ance	action; process	avoidance
-ancy	state or quality	brilliancy
-ant	one who	servant
	thing that	coolant
-ary	having to do with	revolutionary
-ar	of; relating to; like	muscular
-ate	become, make, or cause	activate
	provide with	insulate
	groups	electorate
-action	action; process	presentation
-ative	having; related to	relative
-dom	office or place of	kingdom
	having or being	freedom
-en	having; made up of	woolen
-en	become; cause	sharpen
-ence	state of; action; quality	absence
-ency	state of; quality	efficiency
-er	comparative degree	quicker
-er	one who does a	worker
	certain thing	
	one who lives in a	New Yorker
	certain place	
-ery	place of	bakery
	act of	cookery
	condition of	slavery
-ese	coming from a	Chinese
	certain place	
-ess	feminine form	poetess
-ette	small	kitchenette
-ful	full of; having	hopeful

Table XVII *(continued)*

Suffix	Meaning(s)	Example(s)
-fy	make; make into	petrify
-hood	having the quality or state of	brotherhood
-ial	forms adjectives	celestial
-ic	of; having the quality of	artistic
-ical	forms adjectives	historical
-ician	one who works in a certain field	beautician
-ine	like; composed of	marine
-ine	feminine form of	heroine
-ion	act of; product of	attention
-ious	having	ambitious
-ive	of; tending to be	imaginative
-ize	become; make; cause to be	civilize
-ish	like, having the quality of	foolish
-ism	act; process; condition of	terrorism
-ism	beliefs or teachings of (forms nouns)	realism
-ist	one who	specialist
-itis	disease of; inflammation of	appendicitis
-ity	state of; quality of	acidity
-less	without; not having	hopeless
-let	small	booklet
-like	like	lifelike
-ling	small	duckling
	one who is	hireling
-ly	having the quality of	brotherly
-ty	in a certain way	quality
-ment	action; state of	settlement
-ness	quality of	happiness
-or	one who	actor
-ory	a place	observatory
	of; relating to; involving	sensory
-ous	having; full of	poisonous
-ship	quality or state of	friendship
-ster	one who does or is	youngster

Teaching Prefixes

As with other word attack elements, prefixes and suffixes should be taught inductively. Here is how the prefix **un** might be taught. Suffixes would be taught in similar fashion.

Step 1: Developing the Meaning of the Prefix. Write the word **happy** on the board. Ask students to tell what makes them happy. Put the word **unhappy** on the board. Have students tell about things that make them unhappy. Contrast the words **kind-unkind, true-untrue,** and **afraid-unafraid** in the same way.

Step 2: Determining the Effect of the Prefix. Have students tell how the prefix **un** changed the meanings of **happy, kind, true,** and **afraid.**

Step 3: Generating a Definition for the Prefix. Talk over the words **unhappy, unkind, untrue,** and **unafraid.** Help students see that the prefix **un** in each of these words means **not.** Have students suggest other words that contain the prefix **not.** Write those words on the board and discuss the meaning of each one.

Step 4: Practice. Have students complete practice exercises similar to the ones that follow.

Rewrite the following sentences. For each pair of underlined words, write one word beginning with **un.**

1. The small boy was **not happy.**
2. The boys and girls at the new school were **not friendly.**
3. The rules of the game they played were **not fair.**
4. The sides were **not even.**

Underline the word that fits the meaning of the sentence.

1. Because it had a broken spring, the chair was (comfortable, uncomfortable).
2. Maria fell out of the chair, but she landed on a soft pillow and so she was (hurt, unhurt).
3. The story sounded like a lie, but it was (true, untrue).
4. When it grew dark, the old house was full of strange sounds. Maria felt (afraid, unafraid) and wished her mom and dad were home.

Fill in the blanks with the following words: **uneaten, unhappily, uncertain, unfair.** There will be one word left over.

1. "Does he live on Oak or Walnut St.?" Pat wondered. She was _____. Growing hungry, Pat searched in her pockets for food. She found an _____ apple. At last, Pat found the right house. She rang the bell, but no one answered. "Oh my!" Pat cried _____. "No one is home."

Step 5: Application. Have students read selections that contain prefixes that they have just studied.

Dale and O'Rourke (1971) suggest grouping elements by meaning or function. For example, teach several number prefixes at one time: **mono, uni, bi, tri,** and so forth. Or teach suffixes which change verbs into nouns: **-ance, -ment, -tion.** Affixes that are opposites may also be grouped together. Present **pre-** and **post-** and **-less** and **-ful** at the same time. Because they are opposites, one member of the pair helps define the other. We understand **pre-** better when we compare it with **post-** and vice-versa.

Sequence of Introduction

Prefixes and suffixes that appear in the lowest level of material should be introduced first. The earliest elements taught are inflectional suffixes. In their study of the words contained in eight basal reading series, Harris and Jacobson (1982) found that the inflectional suffixes appeared at the following levels in at least four out of eight basals.

Preprimer: **-s**
Primer: **-ed, -'s, -ing**
Grade two: **-er, -est, -ly**

Tables XVIII and XIX give approximate grade levels for the introduction of prefixes and derivational suffixes. The tables are based on an examination of five leading basals by the author.

TABLE XVIII
Level of Prefixes and Selected Combining Forms

Level	Prefixes
Primary	dis-, pre-, re-, un-
Intermediate	anti-, co-, de-, en-, fore-, il-, im-, in-, ir-, inter-, non-, over-, post-, semi-, sub-, super-
Advanced	ad-, circum-, contra-, counter-, ex-, extra-, out-, sur-

TABLE XIX
Level of Suffixes

Level	Suffixes
Primary	-able, -er, -ible, -ful, -less, -ness, -y
Intermediate	-age, -al, -an, -ant, -en, -ent, -ese, -ess, -est, -ic, -ive, -like, -ment, -or, -our, -some, -th, -tion, -ward
Advanced	-ance, -hood, -ism, -ity, -ize, -osis, -ship

Teaching Root Words and Combining Forms

As with prefixes and suffixes, teaching efforts should concentrate on the most frequently occurring and most useful combining forms and roots. A selected listing of combining forms is contained in Table XX. A listing of common roots is presented in Table XXI.

TABLE XX

Combining Forms

Form	Meaning(s)	Example(s)
audi-, audio-	hearing; sound	audience
auto-	self	autobiography
biblio-	book	bibliography
bio-	life	biology
cardio-, cardi-	heart	cardiologist
cent-, centi-	one hundred	century
chrom-	color	monochrome
chron-	time	chronology
-cide	kill	fratricide
dec-, dek-	ten	decade
deci-	one tenth of	decimal
denti-	tooth	dentist
derma-, derm-	skin	dermatologist
-fer	carry	transfer
ge-, geo-	earth	geology
graph-	something written	autograph
hept-, hepta-	seven	heptagon
kilo-	thousand	kilogram
logo-, log-	word	dialogue
-logy	study of	biology
	expression of	phraseology
macro-, macr-	large	macroorganism
mal-	evil	malice
mega-	great; large	megadollars
	million	megaton
-meter	measure	thermometer
milli-	one thousand	milliped
	one thousandth	millimeter
micr-, micro-	small	microfilm
	making larger	microphone
	one millionth	microwave
mon-, mono-	one; single	monorail
multi-	many; much	multitalented

Table XX *(continued)*

Form	Meaning(s)	Example(s)
ne-, neo-	new	neoclassical
octa-, octo-, oct-	eight	octogon
omni-	all	omnipresent
-onym	name	synonym
pan-	all; including all; everywhere	Pan-American
penta-, pent-	five	pentagon
phon-, phono-	sound; speech	phonograph
-pod	foot	tripod
poly-	many	polygon
pseudo-	not real	pseudonym
quadri-, quadro-, quadru-	four	quadruple
septi-	seven	septillion
sex-	six	sextet
tele-, tel-	distant; far	telephone
tetra-, tetr-	four	tetrapod
thermo-, therm-	heat	thermometer
tri-	three	tricycle

TABLE XXI
Common Roots

Root	Meaning	Example(s)
cred	believe	incredible
dict	say	diction
duct, duc	lead	conduct, deduce
loc	place	location
mit, miss	send	transmit, mission
man	hand	manual
port	carry	import
scrib, script	write	inscribe description
spec	see	spectator
ten	hold	tenacious
vert, vers	turn	reverse, introvert
voc	call	vocal

When teaching root words or combining forms, start with familiar words (Dale & O'Rourke, 1971). For example, when presenting the root

spec, discuss the words **inspector, spectator,** and **prospector.** Lead students to see that all three words contain the root **spec** and that all three words have something to do with **look.** Have students use their knowledge of **spec** to try to determine the meanings of **spectacles** (glasses), **retrospect,** and **introspective.** If students know **retro** and **intro,** they may use this knowledge to help them figure out the words. They may also use context if that is available.

As students come across unfamiliar words that contain the root **spec** or other roots and combining forms that have been presented, lead them to see that the words contain familiar parts, if students don't realize this. Encourage students to make use of these familiar word parts.

The main shortcoming of morphemic analysis is that students fail to apply this valuable tool. Generous provision needs to be made for opportunities for realistic practice and application.

Activities for Reinforcing Morphemic Analysis

• Create displays of related morphemic elements that tie in with a unit of study. For example, when presenting shapes, use your bulletin board to illustrate and label a variety of polygons: **pentagon, hexagon, heptagon, octagon, nonagon,** etc.

• Make use of every opportunity to introduce and/or reinforce knowledge of morphemic elements. When discussing triangles, point out the combining form **tri.** When reading about a triathlon, relate the **tri** in **triathlon** to the **tri** in **triangle** so students can see that both contain the same combining form. Contrast **pentathlon** and **decathlon.**

• Have students create creatures or devices to illustrate knowledge of word parts. For instance, they may create a nonapod or decapod or a heptacycle.

• Display and discuss headlines and news stories that contain useful morphemic elements. The headline may talk about an antiwar group, the birth of quintuplets, the cross-country trip of a quadriplegic, or mention the Pentagon in Washington, D.C.

• Have students collect examples of morphemic elements from their reading.

• Present pertinent morphemic elements when introducing a new topic. When teaching the metric system, for instance, present the elements **milli-, centi-, deci-, deka-, hecto-, kilo-, gram, liter,** and **meter.**

• Have students complete sentences by adding affixes to a root or combining form in exercises similar to the following.

Fill in the blanks by adding combining forms to the combining form **graph** in the sentences below.

1. I asked for Rick Stern's _____graph.
2. Rick Stern gave me a color _____graph of the whole team.
3. I got a copy of Rick's 200-page _____graphy from the library.

To aid in the creating of exercises, words using high frequency prefixes, suffixes, combining forms, and roots are listed at the end of the chapter.

CONTEXT CLUES

When students encounter a printed word that is not in their speaking/listening vocabulary, they may be encouraged to use context to get the meaning of the unfamiliar word. Using a dictionary or glossary would interrupt the flow of the reading and possibly hinder comprehension. Unfortunately, according to research by Schatz and Baldwin (1986), context is not always adequate. It may even suggest an erroneous meaning. McKeown (1985) found that even when clues were explicit, poor readers experienced some difficulty using them.

As Johnson (1981) notes, there are specific thinking processes involved in using context and these vary according to the type of context clues present. Teachers need to do a task analysis of contextual clues and then teach the thinking processes involved.

Johnson postulated a four-step thinking process in the following sentence to arrive at a meaning for **lithium** as used in the following sentence: "We examined samples of mercury, iron, aluminum, and lithium."

> First, they (students) must realize that placement in a series implies some sort of relationship. Second, they must identify each member of the series. Third, they must identify other relationships among the members. Finally, they must draw a tentative conclusion about the unknown member on the basis of the relationships discovered (p. 142).

Teaching Context Clues

Performing the mental operations described by Johnson is not an automatic process. Students need direct instruction and a lot of practice. One way of teaching the use of context clues is by modeling. Emphasis is placed upon showing the thought processes involved. Here is how the process of using items in a series as a context clue might be taught.

Step 1: Explanation of the Concept of Using Context

Explain that often it is possible to get the meaning of an unfamiliar word by noticing how the word is used. Tell the class that this is known as using context clues.

Step 2: Demonstration of Thought Processes

Place the following sentence on the board: "In one section of the store were rows of flutes, clarinets, and oboes." Show the class how you might use context to get the meaning of the word **oboes.** Explain that you looked at the other words in the sentence to see if there were any clues to the meaning of the word. Tell that you noticed that the words **flute, clarinet,** and **oboe** are in a series. Explain that you know that a flute and a clarinet are musical instruments. Your guess is that an oboe is also a musical instrument. Say that you also know that the flute and clarinet are woodwinds. This leads you to believe that the oboe is also a woodwind. Ask the class to check their dictionaries to see if your guess is correct.

Step 3: Cooperative Application of a Context Clue

Place on the board sentences similar to the following, which contain items in a series as a context clue: "Sitting on the dock were crates of oranges, lemons, and **mangoes.**" Discuss possible meanings of the word **mangoes** and the clues that suggest these meanings. Help students to see that oranges, lemons, and mangoes are in a series and that oranges and lemons are fruit so that maybe mangoes are a fruit, too.

Step 4: Practice

Have students complete practice exercises similar to the one listed below. After an exercise has been completed, discuss answers. Place emphasis on guiding students' thinking processes.

Read the following sentences. Notice how the bold word is used in each sentence. Then circle the definition that best fits the bold word.

1. My pen pal in Australia enjoys soccer, tennis, and **cricket.**
         a. hobby   b. sport   c. food
2. Australia is the home of the kangaroo, koala, and the **wombat.**
         a. plant   b. tribe   c. animal
3. Pines, oaks, and **wattles** can be seen in Australia.
         a. trees   b. rocks   c. snakes

Step 5: Application

Students should apply skills to basal readers, content area books, and other reading material. Get in the habit of choosing two or three difficult words that have adequate context clues from students' reading selections. Have students use context clues to get the meanings of the words. Discuss the meanings that they have obtained and the clues that they used. Emphasize the thinking skills involved. Give guidance as necessary.

After students have mastered the items-in-a-series context clue, present other types. Stress the thinking processes involved in using the various types of clues. Some of the major types of context clues are listed below. These categories have been adapted from Dale and O'Rourke (1971). However, it should be noted that the list is not all inclusive and some kinds of contextual clues do not lend themselves to classification.

Types of Context Clues

Definition

The difficult word is defined. A **yurt** is a small circular tent with a rounded top made of animal skins.

Apposition

A noun or clause coming immediately after a difficult word gives the word's meaning. This clue is a form of definition. In the distance we spotted a **zebu,** an Asian ox.

Comparison/Contrast

The meaning of the difficult word is suggested because it is compared or contrasted with a familiar word or phrase. The words **but** or **however** sometimes signal the coming of a word that has an opposite or contrasting meaning. Bill is talkative, but his twin sister Myrna is **taciturn.**

Items in a Series

Familiar words in a series suggest the meaning of an unfamilar word contained in that same series. On my way home I picked up some potatoes, spinach, and **yams.**

Synonym

A synonym of the difficult word may appear in the same sentence or a nearby one. Tired after the long day's march, the **weary** travelers were glad to get home.

Summary

The details in a sentence or series of sentences suggest the meaning of a difficult word. I hadn't eaten all day. All I could think about was food. Even vegetables looked good to me. I was **famished.**

Tone

The tone or mood of the selection suggests the meaning of the unfamiliar word. The sky was dark gray. A steady rain beat upon the window pane. A chill wind whistled through the forest. It was a **dreary** day.

USING THE DICTIONARY

The word attack skill of last resort is the dictionary. When phonics, syllabication, morphemics, and contextual clues fail to yield the meaning and/or pronunciation of an unfamiliar word, students must turn to the dictionary. Dictionary usage tends to be poorly learned and/or poorly taught. It isn't unusual to find high school students and even college freshmen who can't or don't use a pronunciation key and who choose a definition for an unfamiliar word because it is the first definition and not because it fits the way the word is used. Using a dictionary effectively involves being able to apply three major skills: locating the word to be looked up, finding the best definition, and pronouncing the word properly.

Locating the Word

In the largest dictionaries, there are as many as 500,000 words. An abridged dictionary may contain 5,000 to 50,000 words or more. Students need to be able to find a word quickly. Students should know alphabetical order. This skill should be internalized and automatic. Students shouldn't have to recite the whole alphabet to themselves to figure out where the letter **s** falls.

It is helpful if students can turn to the approximate section as soon as they open up a dictionary. A thumb index is helpful for this. Students might also be taught that if the typical dictionary were divided into quarters, here is where the letters of the alphabet would fall:

First quarter	a — d
Second quarter	e — l
Third quarter	m — s
Fourth quarter	t — z

Students should also be taught to use guide words. Many students waste time paging through the dictionary because they fail to make use of guide words. Provide periodic practice in this skill by having dictionary races in which students see how fast they can locate a series of words. For slow students you might obtain a base rate by having them see how long it takes to locate and write down the page numbers for ten words. After instruction and guided practice, have students time themselves as they look up new lists of words. Have them keep a chart of their progress.

Students also need to be taught certain rules of alphabetizing. Listed below are three main rules.

Abbreviations—Are placed according to abbreviated spellings. The abbreviation **pt.** for **pint** follows **psychotic.**

Mc—Placed as though it were spelled Mac.

Numbers—Placed as though spelled out. **4-H** is found under **f.**

Students sometimes have difficulty locating words that contain affixes. They must learn that for the sake of economy separate entries are not always made for each addition of a prefix or suffix. Since the word **jump**'s endings are formed in a predictable manner, there are no separate entries for **jumps, jumped,** or **jumping.** There are entries for **un-** and **afraid** but none for **unafraid.**

Present students with activities that give them practice in finding entry words. For example, have them find the appropriate entry word for each of the following:

unbiased	secretaries
swiftly	twisted
unappreciated	timbers
secretly	unidentified
hopelessly	marshes

Don't overestimate the importance of locational skills. The overall purpose of using a dictionary is to obtain the meanings of unfamiliar words. Undue amounts of time devoted to guide word exercises might be better spent finding the meanings of difficult words that appeared in content area or trade books.

Getting Meanings

Teach students that dictionaries explain the meaning of a word in a variety of ways. For each word, at least one definition will be given.

Often the word will be used in an illustrative sentence and synonyms may be supplied. Some words are illustrated with a drawing or photograph.

Initially have students obtain the meanings of words that have only one or two definitions. Include words for which the dictionary or glossary you are using supplies example sentences, synonyms, antonyms, or illustrations so that students can get a variety of information. Words similar to the following might be used:

punctual	toffee
condor	wrath
equip	zinnia
satchel	tote
portico	tornado

The most difficult but most important dictionary skill is selecting the definition that fits the way an unfamilar word is used in context. Many students, when faced with an entry that has several definitions, will choose the first. They fail to realize that a match must be made between a word's definition and the way the word is used in context. To provide practice with this skill, give students sentences that contain words that have multiple meanings. Start with words whose definitions vary greatly. One possibility is to begin with homographs. Homographs are words whose spellings are the same, but the words have different meanings and may also have different origins. Each homograph usually has a separate entry followed or preceded by a superscript. The word **bay,** for instance, may have five to seven or more entries. In a sense, each entry represents a different word. Here is how the concept of homographs or multiple meanings might be presented.

Step 1: Introducing Homographs

Place the following sentences on the board:

1. We fished in the bay until noon.
2. The hounds will bay at any animal that comes close.
3. My favorite horse was a large bay mare.

Have each sentence read. Discuss with students the fact that **bay** has a different meaning in each sentence. Tell students that words that have the same spelling but different meanings are homographs.

Step 2: Determining Meanings

Have students tell what they think the word **bay** means in each sentence. Write their definitions on the board and have them verified by checking in the dictionary. Point out that **bay** is actually a number of different words with entirely different meanings. Stress the need to use context to select the correct meaning for a word. Using other homographs and/or words with multiple meanings, model and discuss the process of selecting appropriate definitions.

Step 3: Practice

Have students complete exercises similar to the following.

Look at the meanings of the homograph. Then notice how each bold homograph is used in the sentences below. Above each bold homograph, write the number of the meaning that fits best.

1. bark   n.   sound made by a dog
2. bark   n.   outer covering of a tree
3. bark   n.   a sailing ship

Hearing the dog's **bark**, I looked up and saw a large **bark** floating down the river. Rushing through the forest to get a better look, I brushed against the **bark** of a large elm.

Look at the word **house** and its meanings. Then notice how **house** is used in each of the sentences that follow. On the blank, write the number of the meaning that best fits the way **house** is used.

> house   n. 1. A building where people live. 2. The number of people who have come to see a show. 3. A business. 4. A group that makes laws.

____1. The **House** passed a new tax law today.

____2. The movie played to a packed **house**.

____3. We have ten people in our family, so we need a large **house**.

____4. Our class visited a publishing **house**.

Deriving the Correct Pronunciation

Technically, students don't need to know how to pronounce a word in order to be able to read it. All they need to be able to do is to understand it. For example, a reader could pronounce **colonel** as /KOL uh nul/ but understand the word to indicate a rank in the army. However, the word won't become a part of the student's speaking/listening vocabulary unless the student learns the correct pronunciation.

Using the dictionary to get the correct pronunciation of a word involves being able to use a pronunciation key, interpret phonetic respellings, and interpret accents. Students are ready to learn how to use a pronunciation key once they have finished basic phonics, which is usually by the end of second grade.

In teaching the pronunciation key, introduce a few easy elements first. Over time, introduce more complex elements.

Here is a possible sequence:

1. All consonants except /ng/, /**th**/, and /th/; short vowels
2. Remaining consonants and long vowels
3. /o͞o/, /o͝o/, /oi/, /ow/, and /aw/
4. /ə/ and r-vowels

After introducing the consonants and short vowels of the pronunciation key, write brief messages in phrases in phonetic respellings and have students decode them. Some messages might include:

blak kat

jim klas

wun sent

pak uv gum

kik a kan

As more elements are introduced, use them to make longer and more complex phrases and sentences. Eventually compose whole messages in phonetic respellings.

Stress

As part of using the pronunciation key, students must learn how to interpret accent marks. There are three kinds of accent or stress: primary, secondary, and weak or unstressed syllables. Primary stress is usually shown by a high vertical mark. Secondary stress is signified by a low vertical mark or a smaller vertical mark. The stressed syllable may also be printed in boldface. The unstressed syllable is not marked.

To present the concept of stress, follow these steps.

Step 1: Introducing the Concept of Stress. Say a series of two-syllable words similar to the following:

drag′ on	ex ist′
hope′ less	gi raffe′
fair′ ly	in dent′
fi′ nal	in form′
gall′ ant	mis deed′
hin′ der	lo′ cal

Emphasize the accented syllables. Have students listen for the syllable that is said with more stress.

Step 2: Becoming Familiar with Accent Marks. Write the above words on the board with their phonetic respellings. Use the marks contained in the dictionary your class is using, but explain that different dictionaries use different marks. Point out the accent marks. Have students read the words, saying the stressed syllables with more force. Gradually introduce three- and four-syllable words and secondary stress.

Step 3: Practice. Have students complete exercises similar to the following:

Take a look at both the stress marks and the respellings of the words in parentheses. Underline the correct pronunciation.

1. I'll be ready in a _____ (min′ it, mī noot′).
2. After the big meal everyone was feeling _____. (kon′ tent, kən tent′).
3. Lettuce is found in the _____ (prō′ dōōs, prə dōōs′) department.
4. The lawyer will _____ (prez′ ənt, pri zent′) the case next week.
5. The judges said there must be a recount _____ (ri kownt′, rē′ kownt) of the votes.

Step 4: Application. Encourage students to use glossaries or dictionaries to obtain the stress patterns and correct pronunciations of unfamiliar words that they meet. Discuss with students the pronunciation they have obtained in order to make sure that they have gotten the correct pronunciation. Encourage students to use new words in conversation as well as in their writing.

Reinforcement Activities

• Each week have students write five new words on notecards. On one side of the notecard, have them write the word, the context in which it was used, where they saw or heard the word, and what they think the word means. On the other side of the card, have students write the appropriate dictionary definition of the word and its phonetic respelling. Have students exchange cards and quiz each other periodically.

• Explain to students that the following words have more than one pronunciation. Have them use the dictionary and copy the phonetic respelling of the pronunciation they use.

automobile	either
root	tomato
route	

• Have students use the dictionary to help them draw pictures of any five of the following. Students may have to look in more than one dictionary to find meanings.

> yurt
> travois
> trapezoid
> quill
> pentagon
> kelp
> goatee

• Have students pretend they are ordering the following items in a restaurant. Have them use the dictionary to get the pronunciation of the words.

> quiche
> mousse
> antipasta

• Have students answer the following questions using the dictionary to look up any words they don't know.

1. Are you nocturnal or diurnal?
2. Are you taciturn or loquacious?
3. Are you an optimist or a pessimist?
4. Are you conscientious or lackadaisical?
5. Are you haughty or humble?

WORD LISTS

Words Containing Prefixes

co-	con-	counter-
coauthor	concurrent	counteract
cocaptain	condominium	counterattack
coworker	conference	counterclockwise
copilot	confide	countermeasure
copartner	conflict	counterbalance
coequal	congregation	counterintelligence
coeducational	conjunction	countermarch
coincidental	concur	counterpart
coexist	condolence	counteroffensive
cohabit	confirm	countercheck

de-

deforest
defrost
dehumidify
decentralize
deaccelerate
decolonize
decrease
deactivate
demerit
devalue

en-

encase
encircle
enclose
encode
encompass
encourage
enroll
enlarge
enplane
enrich

il-

illegal
illegible
illogical
illiterate
illiteracy
illimitable
illicit
illiberal
illogical

dis-

disagree
disappear
disallow
disbelief
discontent
discontinue
dishonesty
disorder
disobedience
disadvantage

ex-

ex-president
ex-player
ex-teacher
ex-official
ex-actor
ex-owner
ex-senator
ex-captain
ex-announcer
ex-governor

im-

impolite
impossible
imperfect
impersonal
impractical
improbable
improper
immature
impossible

in-

incomplete
indistinct
inexact
inexpensive
informal
inefficient
indefinite
inaccurate
incompetent
inconvenience

inter-

interconnect
intercontinental
interdependent
interchange
intercollegiate
interconnect
intercontinental
interaction
intergalactic
intermission

ir-

irrational
irregular
irrelevant
irresistible
irresponsible
irretrievable
irreversible
irrevocable
irrefutable
irreparable

mis-

mispronounce
misread
misuse
misinform
misjudge
misfortune
misfile
misbelief
misbehavior
miscalculate

non-

nonfiction
nondrying
nonfreezing
nonpublic
nonprofit
nonsmoker
nonresident
nonworker
nontaxable
nonvisual

pre-
preheat
prewinter
pretax
prehistoric
prearrange
predetermine
preview
preemployment
pretest
pregame

pro-
pro-American
probaseball
proboycott
procity
proeducation
proempire
proenvironment
profarmer
prorailroad
protax

post-
postgame
postwar
posttest
postdate
postpone
postorbit
postoperation
postscript
posthypnotic

re-
reread
recheck
recoach
reheat
retype
repaint
resell
repay
replace

semi-
semicircle
semiannual
semifinal
semigloss
semiprivate
semipro
semiprecious
semitropics
semitrailer
semiskilled

sub-
subway
submarine
subcommittee
subbasement
subgroup
subhuman
subcategory
subconscious
subtopic
subcommittee

super-

superhen
superhighway
superstar
superpower
supersonic
superhuman
supercharger
superfine
supertanker
supersensitive

over-

overage
overconfident
overcrowded
overweight
overspend
overestimate
oversleep
overcautious
overdue
overpaid

trans-

transoceanic
transAtlantic
transcontinental
translate
transplant
transport
transform
translucent
transmission
transfer

un-

unhappy
unfriendly
unfair
unlucky
untrue
uncertain
unclear
untie
uncover
undo

uni-

unicycle
unisex
unidirectional
unicorn
uniform
unison
unitary
unipolar
unilateral
univalue

Words Containing Suffixes

-able
agreeable
favorable
laughable
payable
manageable
profitable
reasonable
removable
believable
comfortable

-ible
horrible
terrible
visible
responsible
contemptible
visible
audible
incredible
legible
collectible

-ance
appearance
clearance
acceptance
assistance
disturbance
importance
inheritance
observance
performance
resistance

-ant
assistant
claimant
accountant
descendant
informant
servant
immigrant
coolant
lubricant
sealant

-age
usage
stoppage
shortage
mileage
baggage
breakage
courage
leakage
percentage
postage

-al
actual
original
accidental
alphabetical
biographical
brutal
central
political
seasonal
personal

-ary (n)	**-ary (adj.)**
boundary	elementary
dictionary	imaginary
glossary	dietary
summary	momentary
dignitary	complementary
emissary	customary
intermediary	preliminary
itinerary	complimentary
luminary	military
infirmary	budgetary

-en (adj.)	**-en (v.)**
woolen	cheapen
wooden	freshen
golden	weaken
mistaken	quicken
oaken	sharpen
ashen	lengthen
waxen	shorten
earthen	straighten
molten	darken
silken	moisten

-ence	**-er**
difference	worker
occurrence	dancer
obedience	farmer
reference	grocer
existence	rancher
subsistence	ranger
correspondence	passenger
audience	trainer
circumference	carpenter
dependence	grocer

-ful

spoonful
thankful
fearful
glassful
hopeful
joyful
playful
forgetful
useful
watchful

-ic

comic
historic
phonic
characteristic
cubic
democratic
elastic
encyclopedic
enthusiastic
poetic

-ial

essential
financial
influential
judicial
official
partial
presidential
residential
sequential
superficial

-ity

activity
capability
curiosity
ability
possibility
enormity
formality
generosity
hostility
locality

-ion

comparison
conclusion
decision
suspicion
possession
television
expression
explosion
invasion
division

-ive

active
imaginative
creative
disruptive
effective
conclusive
consecutive
impressive
secretive
distinctive

-ist

artist
typist
motorist
chemist
extremist
nationalist
royalist
scientist
realist
antagonist

-ize

capitalize
magnetize
apologize
specialize
memorize
generalize
summarize
energize
penalize
visualize

-less

careless
helpless
hopeless
cheerless
endless
fearless
hairless
penniless
sleepless
worthless

-ment

agreement
enjoyment
argument
amazement
assignment
contentment
embarrassment
confinement
resentment
replacement

-ness

darkness
fairness
goodness
illness
sadness
likeness
happiness
heaviness
emptiness
wilderness

-or

actor
author
counselor
director
governor
inspector
instructor
supervisor
educator
creator

-ous

dangerous
humorous
joyous
nervous
suspicious
thunderous
victorious
adventurous
courageous
furious

-tion

imagination
description
observation
examination
transportation

explanation
suggestion
punctuation
occupation
pronunciation

-y (n)

army
honesty
armory
bully
baby
economy
antiquity
crony

-y (adj.)

cloudy
chilly
dusty
oily
feathery
cranky
faulty
frosty

-y (little or valued)

kitty
mommy
daddy

Words Containing Combining Forms

audi-, audio-

audience
auditorium
audio
audible
audiometer
audiovisual
audition
audit
auditor
auditory

auto-

autobiography
autograph
automobile
automotive
automatic
automation
autocrat
autonomic
autonomous
autosuggestion

bio-
biology
biography
biochemistry
biophysics
bionic
biosphere
bioluminescence
biopsy
biotic
biodegradable

deca-
decade
decameter
decapod
December
decagon

deci-
decimeter
deciliter
decimal
decimate
decibel

ge-, geo-
geography
geology
geodesic
geomagnetic
geophysics

graph-
autograph
photograph
biography
paragraph
oceanographer
geography
lithographer
monograph
seismography
digraph

kilo-
kilogram
kiloliter
kilowatt
kilocalories
kilocycle

-meter
thermometer
speedometer
odometer
barometer
diameter
perimeter
hexameter
anemometer
altimeter
micrometer

micr-, micro-

microscope
microwave
microfilm
microbiology
microgroove
micrometer
microprojector
microsecond
microbe
microfiche

mid-

midnight
midpoint
miday
midstream
midsummer
midweek
midwinter
midyear
midpost
midline

milli-

millimeter
milliliter
milligram
millisecond
millivolt

mono-

monorail
monoplane
monosyllable
monotone
monolingual

monogram
monologue
monograph
monophonic
monocular

multi-

multicolored
multivolume
multimillionaire
multivitamin
multilingual
multitalented
multiform
multispeed
multivoiced
multiangular

octa-, octo-

octagon
octopus
octapod
octameter
octosyllabic
octave
octet
octogenerian
octillion
octane

omni-

omnipresent
omnipotence
omnifarious
omniscient
omnivorous

penta, pent-

pentagon
pentameter
pentathlon
pentadactyl
pentagular

phono

phonograph
telephone
megaphone
microphone
saxophone
phonetic
symphony
symphonic
phonics
cacophony

poly-

polysyllabic
polygon
polyphonic
polytonal
polyunsaturated
polychrome
polyglot
polygraph
polytechnic
polyclinic

tele-, tel-

television
telephone
telegraph
telegram
telecast
telephoto
telescope
telecommunications
telepathy
telemeter

tri-

triangle
tricycle
triplet
tricolor
trilingual
trimotor
trimonthly
tripod
triad
trifocals

Words with Roots

cred-

credentials
credibility
credible
credit
creditable
incredible
credulous
incredulous
credence
credulity

dict-

dictate
dictation
dictum
dictator
diction
dictionary
edict
interdict
predict
verdict

duct, duc-

abduct
aqueduct
conduct
deduct
induct
introduce
produce
production
reduce
deduce

loc-	man-
local	manage
locale	manacle
localism	management
locality	maneuver
locally	manicure
locate	manipulate
location	manuscript
locator	manual
	manufacture

CHAPTER VIII

TEACHING WORD ATTACK SKILLS
TO DISABLED LEARNERS

ALTHOUGH the majority of students learn phonics and related decoding skills with relative ease, a fairly large number of youngsters have difficulty learning or applying phonics skills. Some lack adequate readiness for phonics. Others overuse phonics. Some do well with single-syllable phonics but can't seem to apply these skills to multisyllabic words. A few youngsters have such poor associative word-learning ability that they need specialized word-learning techniques. This chapter provides suggestions for handling these and other decoding difficulties.

DIFFICULTY MASTERING READINESS SKILLS

Many youngsters have difficulty learning phonics because they have poor auditory or visual discrimination or are unable to grasp language metalinguistically. This means they have a problem dealing with language on an abstract level and so are unable to separate sounds from words. They can't detect rhyme because they can't abstract the ending sounds of words. They have difficulty learning beginning sounds because they can't abstract the beginning sound from the rest of the word. They can't abstract /b/ from **bat**, for example. The traditional activities found in most programs are too advanced for these youngsters and also fail to provide sufficient reinforcement. Programs which might be used to help these students include those by Rosner (1975), Elkonin (1973), and Hillerich and Johnson (1986).

Rosner's Approach

To help youngsters who are having difficulty abstracting sounds from words, Rosner offers a five-level program that begins with dissecting the components of compound words and ends with perceiving initial and final consonants. Before students begin the program, they take a brief test which places them in the appropriate level of proficiency. Students are then instructed at that level. The five levels of the program are described below.

Level 1

The student learns to identify the words in a compound word and then deletes a word from a compound word. At first, the student claps each time he hears the separate words within the compound word. The student would clap for the **foot** and **ball** in **football.** Later, the child draws dashes instead of clapping when he hears the words in a compound word. Other activities include omitting a word from the compound and/or identifying the omitted word. The teacher says **football** and then says **ball.** The students must tell what word was left out. The student is also asked to repeat a compound word and is then asked to say the word without one of its parts. For example, the teacher asks the child to say **sunshine** and then say **sunshine** without the **sun** or without the **shine.**

Level 2

Level 2 activities are identical to those of Level 1 except that three-syllable words are used instead of compounds. Students, for example, would clap their hands or draw dashes and then identify and omit syllables in words like **apartment, hospital,** and **October.**

Level 3

Level 3 begins with having the child hear the beginning sound of a word. The child is instructed to say the word **sat.** The teacher then asks if the word **sat** begins with the /s/ sound. Both words beginning with /s/ and those beginning with other sounds are presented. Later, the child is instructed to say the missing sound and then omit the sound from key words. For instance, the child is told to say **sat** and then **at.** The child is asked to tell what sound is missing in **at** that was heard in **sat.** The child is also directed to omit the initial sound. The youngster is asked to say **sat** and then say it again without the /s/ sound.

Level 4

Level 4 is identical to Level 3 except that the focus in on final sounds.

Level 5

Level 5 involves working with medial vowel and consonant sounds.

Students who can complete Level 3 are ready for instruction in letter-sound relationships. They can perceive and abstract the beginning sounds of words, which is the primary prerequisite for phonics instructions. There is no need for instruction in Levels 4 and 5.

Elkonin Technique

According to Elkonin (1973), a Russian researcher, being able to analyze the sounds of words "is the most important prerequisite for the successful learning of reading and writing" (p. 571).

To help students learn this essential skill, Elkonin devised and tested a technique that would objectify or "materialize" the skill. The child is presented with a picture and markers or chips. Beneath the picture is a series of squares that contains the same number of blocks as there are phonemes in the word represented by the picture and places a marker in each square as he says each phoneme. For example, a drawing of a cat would have three squares drawn under it. The child would look at the picture, say /k/, /a/, /t/ and upon pronouncing each phoneme would place a marker in a square.

As explained by Elkonin, the value of the drawing is that it focuses the child's mind on the word. A spoken word might be forgotten. The squares tell the child that he must find three sounds. Placing the markers in the squares helps the child realize that the sounds must be said in order. Although the letters of the word could have been used instead of squares, Elkonin feels this might detract from the auditory nature of the task.

In order to complete the task successfully, students must be taught to stress and/or draw out each sound. Teachers should work closely with students until the youngsters are able to do this. The teachers should initially present words that have just two or three sounds. It is also important to work with words that are in the child's listening/speaking vocabulary and that are easily depicted. Possible practice words include the following:

bee	fish	bed
key	foot	cake
pie	leaf	bag
tie	pen	soap
cat	pan	hat

bat	nail	cup
dog	rat	rope
bell	ring	bus
book	moon	rake
boat	sun	mop

In time, students should be able to dispense with the squares and the markers. Give students illustrations of words, have them say the words and then tell how many sounds the words have. Once students have mastered this activity, they might be asked to tell how many sounds are in words spoken by the teacher. At this point, students should also be able to tackle auditory discrimination/perception of initial sounds in preparation for learning letter-sound relationships.

Hillerich and Johnson's Approach

Hillerich and Johnson's program, *Ready Steps* (1986), is a readiness for readiness program. *Ready Steps* builds basic skills needed to enter traditional readiness programs. *Ready Steps* builds auditory discrimination of beginning sounds by having children play a series of games that involve working with words that have the same medial and ending but different beginning sounds. For instance, the teacher tells a child that she is going to play a game with her name. After Jan, the student, says her name, the teacher asks: "Is your name Pan?" The child says no and gives the correct pronunciation of her name. In another game, the teacher holds up a pen and says: "I call this a **hen.** Did I say the name right? What would you call it?" Other activities involve asking students to tell if they would sail on a boat or a coat, point to a picture of a cake when shown a cake and a rake, and tell whether they would eat a pie or a tie.

Additional Readiness Activities

Students aren't really ready for formal phonics instruction until they can perceive beginning sounds. To help students perceive beginning sounds, have them listen to alliterative stories and recite tongue twisters. After students have been working with alliterative stories and tongue twisters for a time, lead them to see that many of the words begin with the same sound. Help students become aware of the beginning sounds of their given names. Say a student's name, omitting the first sound. Have the class pronounce the child's whole given name. Discuss the fact that the first sound was left off.

Give students a number of phonograms. Have them create words by adding beginning sounds. For example, have students add sounds to /ē/ (**bee, key, see, tea, we**) or at (**bat, cat, fat, rat, sat**).

FAILURE TO READ FOR MEANING

When phonics and/or oral reading is overemphasized, students sometimes use phonics to the exclusion of other clues. They concentrate so hard on translating letters into sounds that they don't notice that what they're reading has no meaning. Their oral reading is characterized by nonsense words and words that fail to make sense in context. These students may not realize that the main purpose of reading is to obtain meaning. Stress this point with them. Show them how to use context along with phonics to decode words. Have them monitor their reading so that if they produce a nonsense word, they then try alternative pronunciations until they construct a real word. Stress comprehension. Emphasize the importance of being able to tell what happened in a story rather than being able to pronounce each word.

EXCESSIVE SOUNDING OUT

If students have to sound out nearly every word, reading becomes a very laborious process. Comprehension suffers or is nonexistent because so much time and energy are devoted to the decoding process. Provide students with easy trade books or texts in which just about every word is known so that they have the opportunity to become fluent readers. Also use flash cards, tachistoscopic exercises, or other quick recognition activities so that students build up a store of words that they can read instantaneously.

EXCESSIVE DECODING ERRORS

Students who seem to be stumbling over every other word may be grappling with material that is too difficult. Try giving them easier material. Often we underestimate the seriousness of a poor reader's disability. Giving a third grader reading on a first-grade level a 2-1 or 2-2 reader is not an adequate solution. Students need materials that they can handle with relative ease. Students should know nearly all the words in a selection they are about to read. As a rock-bottom minimum, they should be familiar with 95 percent of the words. Research by Gambrell, Wilson, and Gantt (1981) and Berliner (1981) suggests that students make the most progress when they are reading at a level at which 95 to 98 percent of the words are known.

DIFFICULTY LEARNING PHONICS

Most often, the initial course of action for students who experience difficulty learning or applying phonics is to give them added phonics instruction. Sometimes, this is the worst approach. Because of poor auditory perception or inadequate memory or other problems, some students have difficulty with a phonics approach. If students have been carefully taught and have honesly tried but failed to learn, switching to a sight or eclectic approach might be the best tactic. Students no longer have to place so much reliance on weak areas. Now they can make fuller use of context clues to help them decode.

Sometimes just changing programs helps. Students may associate a particular program with failure. Feeling discouraged, they may have given up trying. A fresh approach may help to get them off to a more positive start.

CAN'T KEEP UP WITH THE PROGRAM

Some students need more time to learn decoding skills. You may want to choose a program that is slower paced and/or which offers plentiful reinforcement. To provide added reinforcement, obtain a supply of beginning reader trade books and have students read them at the appropriate times. For instance, after short a has been introduced, encourage students to read trade books that stress this pattern. See "Children's Books That Can Be Used to Reinforce Word Attack Skills" in Chapter XI for a listing of beginning-reader trade books.

DIFFICULTY WITH MULTISYLLABIC WORDS

There are a number of students who do fine with single-syllable phonics but experience serious difficulty decoding multisyllabic words.

There are three related techniques that might be used with these young-sters: Glass analysis, compare/contrast, and pattern analogy.

Glass Analysis

Research by Glass (1973), Gunning (1988), and Rubeck (1977) suggests that students use pronounceable units when decoding a word. These units are generally larger than a single phoneme but smaller than a syllable. The word **branches,** for instance, might be decoded as **br-anch-es, br-an-ches, branch-es,** or **br-anches.**

To capitalize upon this apparently natural tendency to cluster sounds into pronounceable units, Glass (1976) has constructed a system that presents 119 frequently occurring pronounceable units. They are graded into five categories: starters (**at**), medium one (**ed**), medium two (**all**), harder one (**ite**), and harder two (**air**).

These clusters are presented within the context of whole words and are heavily drilled so that students will be conditioned to recognize them automatically as they meet them in their texts. The **ong** cluster is presented below as an example of how the technique works.

Step 1

The teacher gives the cluster in the context of a whole word while holding up a page containing the word. The teacher says: "The word is **song.** What is the word?"

Step 2

The teacher goes from sound to letter. The teacher says, "In the word **song,** what letter makes the /s/ sound? What letters make the /ong/ sound?"

Step 3

The teacher goes from letter to sound. The teacher says, "In the word **song,** what sound does the letter **s** make? What sound does **o-n-g** make?"

Step 4

The teacher removes a sound. The teacher asks, "If I took off the /s/ from the word **song,** what sound would be left?

Step 5

The teacher inquires about the whole word. Pointing to the word **song,** the teacher asks, "What is the whole word?"

Both easy and difficult words are used with the system. After recognizing the **ess** in **bless,** for instance, students go on to recognize the same cluster in **lesson** and **expressive.**

Although the Glass Analysis is recommended for use in decoding multisyllabic words, Glass is firmly against teaching youngsters how to syllabicate. He feels that no one uses syllabication to decode words. Syllabication, according to Glass, is something done after the word has been decoded.

Comparison/Contrast

The comparison/contrast technique as composed by Cunningham (1978) also attempts to have students use pronounceable word parts. Using this strategy, students break an unknown polysyllabic word down into known units. This is done by comparing the polysyllabic word with words or word parts that are familiar to the student. For example, in breaking down the word **employ,** the student would use her knowledge of words like **empty** or **embarrass** to decode the **em** part of **employ.** She would recognize a portion of **ploy** because of her knowledge of **boy** and **toy.** Her store of known words and word parts would both help her to segment the polysyllabic word into pronounceable units and then to assign the correct pronunciation to those units.

Students are taught to use the compare/contrast strategy in a five-step procedure. In the first three steps, students write the following words on index cards: **he, went, her, can, car, in, at, then, it, is, let, fish, sun, big,** and **and.** The words are presented five at a time.

To practice recognizing pronounceable word parts, students are given a list of two-syllable words. Each syllable is similar to one of the words on the index cards. Students are asked to match the words on their index cards with the word parts in the two-syllable words. Thus, when a student sees the word **garment,** she matches it with **car** and **went.** Students start out using five familiar single-syllable words, then ten, and then fifteen.

In Step 4, students are no longer limited to using the fifteen words on index cards. Students examine a series of selected two-syllable words and supply a word for each syllable that is similar to the syllables. Words are drawn from the students' own mental store of words.

In Step 5, students work with words of three or more syllables. Advanced students are also taught syllables such as **tion** and **ous** that occur only in multisyllabic words.

Although a useful technique, the compare/contrast strategy has two weaknesses. First of all, there is a fairly large number of multisyllabic words that contain one or more syllables that aren't similar to one-syllable words. Secondly, sound units sometimes change their pronunciation when they appear in multisyllabic words. For example, the second syllable of the word **market,** which is listed as a practice word by Cunningham (1978) for the words **car** and **let,** is unaccented and so has a schwa pronunciation. However, the word **let,** which is supposed to match up with it, has a short **e** pronunciation. Students using a comparison/contrast strategy would need to adjust pronunciation for some words.

Pattern Analogy

A third approach to teaching disabled learners how to decode multisyllabic words is to teach a pattern analogy technique. In this method, students compare a multisyllabic word with a known single-syllable word. Here is how the open syllable long **a** pattern would be presented.

The teacher would write the following words on the board.

A	B	C
pay	gray	a
paper	gravy	able
labor	navy	table
favor	native	fable
flavor	nation	cable
	nature	

The teacher would ask a volunteer to read the first word in Column A. The teacher would then point out that the second word begins in the same way as the first word and would ask the volunteer or another student to read the second word (paper). If students had difficulty with the word **paper,** the teacher would underline the first syllable and tell them it is pronounced the same way as **pay.** The teacher would then have students attempt to read the whole word, but would supply help as needed. Students would read each succeeding word by comparing it with the word that comes before it. Columns B and C would be done in the same way. The teacher would supply help whenever necessary.

This procedure helps students learn important syllabication patterns. It also helps them to recognize pronounceable units within the context of whole words. See Chapter VI for a listing of syllable patterns that might be used with this approach.

SEVERE WORD-LEARNING PROBLEMS

A small percentage of youngsters experience such severe difficulty learning to decode that they need to be taught with specialized word-learning techniques. These youngsters are characterized by poor memory for words and letters and may also have perceptual problems. They experience great difficulty learning the names of the alphabet, sight words, and sounds represented by letters. They may be taught five sight words and, despite lots of practice, forget all or most of them within a few minutes or by the next day.

These youngsters generally will need one-to-one instruction by a trained reading clinician. They may also need an approach which involves kinesthetic and tactile modalities in addition to visual and auditory ones.

Two of the best-known specialized word learning techniques are the Fernald (1943) and the Gillingham (Gillingham & Stillman, 1960). Although both approaches advocate using four modalities and incorporate tracing in their strategies, the Fernald is a holistic, analytic approach. The Gillingham is a synthetic, sound-by-sound approach.

The Fernald Technique

Fernald and Keller first described their technique in 1921. A fuller description was supplied in 1943. The Fernald technique has four stages. The stages, adapted according to the VAKT version (Johnson and Kress, 1966) are listed below.

Stage 1

The child traces a word with which he has had difficulty. The word is first written on a piece of 4" × 12" paper by the instructor. The word is written in blackboard-size script with a large black crayon in manuscript or cursive. The teacher says the whole word, writes it, says it syllable by syllable, and says the whole word again. The student then begins tracing the word.

Every attempt is made to maintain the integrity of the word. The student doesn't overemphasize or distort sounds but says the word naturally. In tracing the word **hat,** for example, the student would say "hat" before tracing the word, would say "hat" as he began tracing the word but would not elongate the pronunciation or say the word's individual sounds. He would then say "hat" after tracing the word.

A multisyllabic word would be broken into syllables. The student would say the word as a whole and would then trace it in syllables. For the word **volcano,** the student would say "volcano" and then begin tracing. The student would say "vol," "ca," "no," as he began tracing each of the word's three syllables. After completing the tracing, he would then say the whole word.

Tracing is done with the fore and middle finger or with just the forefinger. The student continues tracing until he feels that he knows the word. The student then turns over the sheet of paper containing the traced word. On a sheet of 4" × 12" paper held vertically, the student writes the word from memory twice. The first writing is covered up while the student writes the second one. Each time, after writing the word, the student compares it with the model that the teacher wrote.

If the student has written the word correctly, he files the word alphabetically in a shoe box. If the word has not been written correctly, the student traces until he feels ready to attempt writing the word from memory again.

Successful performance is encouraged. Students are stopped as soon as they start to make a mistake. Words to be traced may be drawn from any source but usually come from an experience story that the student writes. The student traces any word that he is unable to write or read.

As soon as possible, students should see and read a typed list of words that were traced and the experience story in which the words appear. Students need to see typed versions of their words and also can benefit from the additional reinforcement.

Stage 2

Stage 2 is similar to Stage 1, except that the student no longer traces the word. The teacher writes the word on a 3" × 5" card. As in Stage 1, the teacher says the whole word, says it in syllables, and then says the whole word once more. The student says the word, says its parts—if it is a multisyllabic word—and then says the whole word. As in Stage 1, the student demonstrates that he knows the word by correctly writing it twice.

Stage 3

Stage 3 is similar to Stage 2 except that the teacher no longer writes words for the student.

Stage 4

The student needs no special help in learning new words.

VAKT involves heavy use of the dictionary. Before demonstrating the tracing of a word, the teacher looks up the word in question to determine the correct spelling and number of syllables. Gradually the student takes increasing responsibility for looking up words to be learned.

Gillingham Approach

Anna Gillingham (1960) with the help of Bessie Stillman translated Samuel Orton's theories of reading disability into a remedial technique. The Gillingham approach embodies synthetic phonics and is multisensory. Letters and phonograms are presented in three main stages called associations. These stages are described below.

Association 1

The child is shown a card with a letter written on it. The teacher says the name of the letter. The child repeats the name of the letter. After the child has mastered the letter-name association, the teacher says the sound of the letter, which the child repeats.

Association 2

The teacher says the sound of the letter, but doesn't show its printed form. The child gives the name of the letter.

Association 3

The teacher writes the letter as the child watches. The child then traces the letter. Later, the teacher makes the sound represented by the letter and the child writes the letter. The child says the name of the letter as he writes it.

In the above presentations, various associations are made between the visual, auditory, kinesthetic, and tactile modalities. Association 1 lays the groundwork for reading, Association 2 for oral spelling, Association 3 for written spelling.

In the program, individual letter-sound relationships are taught. Individual sounds are then built into words "like bricks into a wall" (Gillingham & Stillman, 1960, p. 40). Key words are also used to teach letter-sound relationships. The child is taught to respond to the **a** card, for example, by saying the word **apple** and the sound /a/.

As students master short-vowel words, they are given *Little Stories,* to read. *Little Stories* are composed of short-vowel words and resemble selections in linguistic readers. In preparation for reading multisyllabic words, students are taught to read syllables such as **sep** or **dit** so that they will recognize these elements when they meet them in polysyllabic words. Other activities include reading words whose syllables have been separated: **help ful, win ter, qui et.** Students also put jumbled syllables together to form words: **ber tim, bor hood neigh, ment a part.**

CHAPTER IX

DIALECT VARIATION AND THE
TEACHING OF PHONICS

DIALECT VARIATION

HOW DO YOU pronounce the following words: **roof, coffee, route?** If you said /rŏŏf/ or /rōōf/, /KAW fē/ or /KO fē/, /rōōt/ or /rowt/, you are correct. Each of the words has at least two acceptable pronunciations.

Variation in pronunciation is occasioned by geographical, social, and even vocational factors. The most readily observable differences are regional. Three major regional dialects have been identified: Northern, Southern, and Midland. Within each region, there is additional variation.

To some people, the word **dialect** suggests a stigma. To them, a dialect is the version of English that other people speak. However, each of us speaks a dialect. As linguist W.N. Francis (1983) noted, "a language spoken by more than a handful of people exhibits the tendency to split into dialects" (p. 1). Lending support to this contention are the citations of dictionary editors. For more than 50 years, the editors of the Merriam-Webster dictionaries have been collecting transcriptions of the speech of educated individuals. Based on these citations, which run into the millions, the editors have concluded that "there is a considerable amount of perfectly acceptable pronunciation variation in the language" (Mish, 1983, p. 33).

Although dialect variation is a fact of language, most reading programs and methods texts ignore these differences and are written as though all words have just one acceptable pronunciation. Before being revised, a standardized reading test asked students to choose the word that had an /aw/ pronunciation. The expected response was **auto.** However, for many youngsters the word **auto** begins with a short **o** pronunciation. In some basal and supplementary phonics programs, the word

egg is used to illustrate the short **e** sound. However, that doesn't work well for youngsters who pronounce the word with a long **a,** which is also an acceptable pronunciation. In some exercises, students are told that **frog** and **dog** rhyme. But, for many students, **frog** has a short **o** pronunciation and **dog** has an /aw/ pronunciation.

Failure to consider dialect variation leads to confusing instruction. Most of us suffer from the Guttenberg syndrome. We believe what we see in print. If our students say /āg/, when the teacher's guide clearly indicates that **egg** begins with a short **e,** we "correct" our students' pronunciation. Since /āg/ is a legitimate pronunciation of **egg,** we should adjust the text to fit the children's dialect and not vice versa. This can be done in a number of ways. First, we might explain that the word **egg** can be pronounced in more than one way. Or we can ignore the exercise or example that contains the confusing item. We might also create exercises that don't contain potentially confusing items. Of course, we can also select materials that do not contain confusing items.

Variable Pronunciations

Listed below are some pronunciations that are frequently interchanged. The list is not an exhaustive one, but it does contain some of the most common occurrences.

/o͞o/ and /o͝o/

Words like **roof** and **room** generally have a long double **o** sound in Northern dialects, except for large cities, and a short **oo** pronunciation in Southern and Midland regions (Reed, 1977).

/o/ and /å/

Most speakers pronounce **father** with a short **o** sound so that it rhymes with **bother.** However, many speakers use a one-dot **a** pronunciation, which is more elongated than the short **o** and is articulated in a position that is farther forward (Reed, 1977).

/aw/ and /o/

According to Reed (1977), one of the most complicated pronunciation variations is use of /o/ and /aw/ in words. Many Northern speakers don't distinguish between these two sounds. These speakers typically use an /o/ rather than an /aw/ sound so that **cot** and **caught** have an identical pronunciation. However, some speakers use /o/ where /aw/ is normally used but also use /aw/ in some words. For example, they may say "lawg" and "dahg" instead of "lawg" and "dawg" or "lahg" and "dahg."

/o͞o/ and /ow/

Words like **route** can be pronounced with a long double **oo** sound, /ro͞ot/, or with an /ow/ sound, /rowt/.

/s/ and /z/

Words like **greasy** can be pronounced with an /s/ or /z/ in its final syllable: /grēsy/ or grēzy/.

NONSTANDARD DIALECTS

Teachers may also need to make adjustments for youngsters who speak nonstandard English. Nonstandard English, in this case, would be pronunciations that do not conform to those of educated speakers of a region. Teachers should note what kinds of sounds youngsters have difficulty with and provide added practice in auditory discrimination when these items are presented, if it is felt that the youngsters' discrimination of these items is not adequate. For example, if youngsters pronounce **these** and **those** as "dese" and "doze" and also experience difficulty discriminating between spoken **those** and **doze,** present exercises similar to those listed below.

Developing Auditory Discrimination

The purpose of the following exercises is to develop sufficient auditory discrimination between /d/ and /th/ or /th/ so that /d/ is recognized as a sound distinct from /th/. Some youngsters may pronounce **these** and **those** as "deze" and "doze" but recognize that **those** and **doze** begin with different sounds. Insofar as reading instruction is concerned, these youngsters need no special help, although instruction might be undertaken for correct usage or speech purposes.

Activity 1

Ask students questions similar to the following:

1. Hold up your thumb and ask: Is this a dumb or a thumb?

2. Hold up a dime and ask: Is this a dime or thyme?
3. Hold up a dump truck and ask: Is this a dump truck or a thump truck?
4. Ask: When you sleep, do you doze or those?
5. Is tomorrow a day or a they?

Activity 2

Read the following word pairs. Have students raise one hand if the words are different and two if they are the same.

those	doze
than	Dan
did	did
they	day
then	den
dime	thyme
den	then
dip	dip
dud	thud
dumb	thumb

BLACK ENGLISH

Black English is a fully formed language that has its own system of syntax, semantics, and phonology. As Labov (1981) comments:

> It is most important for the teacher to understand the relation between standard and nonstandard and to recognize that nonstandard English is a system of rules, different from the standard but not necessarily inferior as a means of communication. (p. 517)

There are more similarities than differences when black English is compared to white English. Both black English and white English have the same number of sounds. As Smitherman (1981) notes:

> Many times Black Dialect sounds tend to be generally similar to those of white speakers of any given region of the country. That is, some black speakers in Boston say **paak the cah** (deleting r's) in the same way as white speakers of that area, and Southern Black Speech sounds pretty much the same as Southern White Speech. As a matter of fact, when you talk about pronunciation there is no national standard even among white speakers, since the regional dialects of the country all have their own individual standards. (p. 522)

Research (Goodman, 1978; Melmed, 1973) suggests that black dialect does not significantly hinder the ability of students to learn to read. In general, students who spoke black dialect had no special difficulty understanding written material. However, in a study of third graders, Melmed (1973) found that black students do have difficulty discriminating between certain word pairs. The greatest difficulty was caused by vowel variation, l'lessness, and simplification of consonant clusters. Black English homophones such as **cole-cold** and **deaf-death** only interfered with comprehension when there was insufficient syntactic or semantic clues: His (pass, past), made him famous.

Shuy (1971) noted a number of phonological characteristics of black English. A partial listing of these characteristics is contained in Table XXII.

TABLE XXII

Phonological Characteristics of Black English

Reduction of Final Consonant Clusters

/st/	rest	res
/sp/	clasp	clas
/sk/	desk	des
/ft/	left	lef
/nd/	hand	han
/ld/	cold	col
/pt/	rapt	rap
/kt/	act	ac

Reduction of Affixed Endings

/sht/	rushed	rush
/zd/	teased	tease
/jd/	judged	judge
/vd/	loved	love
/md/	tamed	tame

Reduction of Final Voiced /b/, /d/, and /g/ to Voiceless /p/, /t/, /k/

/b/	tab — tap
/d/	bud — but
/g/	pig — pik

Other Substitutions

/i/ for /e/ before **n**: **tin** for **ten**

/in/ for /ing/: **runnin'** for **running**

Developing Discrimination

Not all speakers of black English will include all of the features noted in Table XXIII in their speech. However, when presenting phonics, the teacher should be aware of potentially confusing elements and adapt instruction, if necessary. Before teaching ending consonant clusters, for example, teachers should develop auditory discrimination and perception of the cluster by contrasting it with its reduced form so that students become aware of the fully pronounced cluster.

Here is how the **ld** cluster might be presented. The activities are designed to help students discriminate betwen /l/ and /ld/.

Activity 1

Ask the questions listed below:

1. (Holding up a picture of gold) Is this goal or gold?
2. (Holding a bowl) Is this a bowl or a bold?
3. (Shivering or holding up a picture of a winter scene) Is this coal or cold?
4. (Telling the students to stand up) Have I toll or told you to stand up?
5. (Holding up a picture of a mole) Is this a mole or a mold?

Activity 2

Say the following word pairs. Have students raise one hand if the words are different and two if they are the same.

coal	cold
hole	hold
bowl	bold
sole	sold
told	told
foal	fold
goal	goal
roll	rolled
toll	told

Conduct similar auditory exercises with other items that lend themselves to confusion. Use the following lists as an aid to creating exercises.

Final Consonants

b — p	d — t	g — k
tab — tap	mud — mutt	pig — pick
cab — cab	had — hat	bag — back
cup — cup	bud — bud	rag — rag
gab — gap	bad — bat	tug — tuck
lip — lip	mad — mat	wag — whack
slab — slap	had — had	dug — duck
rib — rip	pad — pat	peg — peck
bib — bib	sad — sat	rag — rack
cab — cap	bid — bit	hag — hack
cub — cup	kid — kid	tug — tug

Consonant Clusters

n — nd	s — st
ban — band	lease — least
bran — brand	pass — past
fen — fend	miss — miss
fine — fined	worse — worst
fun — fun	Russ — rust
men — mend	last — last
mine — mind	muss — must
ten — ten	guess — guest
win — wind	chess — chest
wan — wand	loss — lost

Teaching -in or -en Words

When presenting the **-in** or **-en** pattern, adapt instruction to fit students' pronunciation of these items. You may wish to tell students that some speakers change the pronunciation of short **e** to a short **i** when it is followed by an **n.** Omit or alter text activities that may be confusing. Do not attempt to change students' pronunciation to fit a particular workbook exercise.

Acceptance

Above all, be accepting of every child's dialect. Remember that the child's dialect serves him or her well in his speech community and is the variation of English spoken by friends and loved ones. Remember, too, that phonics is a means to an end and not an end in itself. The ultimate objective of reading is understanding not pronunciation. Being able to pronounce the words in standard dialect is not a prerequisite for understanding the words, although it may be a prerequisite for vocational mobility at some later date.

Importance of Attitude

The most important factor in handling nonstandard or variant dialects is teacher attitude. Goodman and Goodman (1978) analyzed the oral reading of four groups who spoke low status dialects: Downeast Maine, Appalachian White, Mississippi Rural Black, and Hawaiian Pidgin. Although the authors felt that the most notable evidence of dialect influence was phonological, they concluded that "There's no evidence of dialect miscues affecting comprehension or of dialect factors which would interfere with learning to read. The possible exception. . .is the effect of teacher attitudes." (p. 82).

According to linguist-anthropologist Burling (1970), all English speakers have a number of homonyms in their speech (**hour—our, buy—by**). However, speakers of black dialect simply have additional homonyms. "They will give him serious problems," says Burling, "only if his teacher fails to understand that these words are homonyms in the child's natural speech." (p. 125) Burling cautions against confusing the child by unnecessarily correcting him.

> If a student sees the word **death** and reads /def/, he is correctly interpreting the symbols into his natural pronunciation and deserves to be congratulated. If his teacher insists on correcting him and telling him to say /deth/, she is pronouncing a sequence of sounds that is quite literally foreign to the child, and he may even have trouble hearing the difference between his own and his teacher's versions. Unwittingly, the teacher is correcting the child's pronunciation instead of his reading skills. (p. 125)

CHAPTER X

TEACHING PHONICS TO NONNATIVE SPEAKERS OF ENGLISH

BASED ON THE 1980 census, approximately 17 percent of school-age children come from homes in which a language other than English is spoken. Moreover, that percentage is expected to rise (Levin, 1985). In some large school districts, there may be a dozen different languages or more spoken. Students' languages may include such diverse tongues as Spanish, Chinese, Italian, French, Polish, Korean, Thai, or Vietnamese. Regardless of language spoken, students are not ready for instruction in reading English until they can comprehend spoken English on at least a rudimentary level.

Students who are proficient readers in another language generally transfer skills to reading English and make rapid progress. Students who are not literate in their native tongue need instruction in beginning reading skills. If possible, these students should be taught to read in their native tongue first.

Phonics instruction may pose special difficulties for nonnative speakers of English who are learning to read English. In many languages there is a close fit between symbol and sound. In Spanish, for example, most letters represent one sound only. Conversely, most sounds are spelled in just one way. Learning to read English can be a shock for youngsters used to a one-to-one correspondence between symbol and sound. English has a highly variable spelling system. Students need to learn to make the most of the regularities of English and to adapt a flexible decoding strategy so if one pronunciation for a particular spelling doesn't produce a word that makes sense in context, then it is necessary to try a second and, sometimes, a third pronunciation.

Students literate in another language also need to be aware that some of the letter-sound relationships which they learned from their native

173

tongue may not apply to English. For example, in Spanish the letter **a** represents a short **o** as in **aqua.** However, in English this letter most frequently stands for short **a** as in **hat.**

The most difficult obstacle for nonnative speakers of English, however, is the difference between phonologies. Often there will be speech sounds in English that are not a part of the child's native language. In Spanish, for example, there are twenty-eight speech sounds. In English, there are approximately forty-one sounds.

Because of these and other language differences, it is necessary for the teacher to make some adjustments when teaching phonics and other word attack skills to nonnative speakers. First of all, the teacher should be aware of some of the major differences between English and the student's native language. Once these differences are known, the teacher is then in a position to adapt instruction to meet the students' needs.

It is beyond the scope of this text to detail crucial difference between the phonologies of English and other languages. However, because Spanish is the second most frequently spoken language in the United States, some differences between English and Spanish sound systems are described in the following pages.

DIFFERENCES BETWEEN SPANISH AND ENGLISH

Spanish is a reading teacher's delight. Unlike English in which 41 sounds may be spelled in 300 or more ways, Spanish has a highly predictable spelling-sound system. There are fewer vowels in Spanish than there are in English, but vowels play a more prominent role in Spanish. According to Nash (1977), vowels occur 56.4 percent of the time and consonants 43.6 percent. In English, the proportion of occurrence between vowels and consonants is reversed. Vowels appear only 37.4 percent of the time whereas consonants occur 62.6 percent of the time (Nash, 1977).

In English, consonant letter-sound correspondences are less variable and, for that reason, are often introduced first in phonics instruction. In Spanish, however, vowels are more predictable than consonants.

Vowel Differences

Spanish lacks a short **i (sit),** short **a (cat),** short **u (cup),** short double **o (book),** and schwa **(sofa),** which is the most frequently occurring English vowel sound. In addition, some of the vowel sounds shared by the two languages may vary slightly in pronunciation. For example, the sound symbolized by **au** in **fauna** in Spanish is very similar to but not identical to the sound represented by **ow** in **cow**. A comparative listing of Spanish and English vowels is contained in Table XXIII.

TABLE XXIII
English and Spanish Vowels

English		Spanish
/a/	hat	_____
/e/	net	perro
/i/	it	_____
/o/	hot	gato
/u/	cup	_____
/ā/	cake	pelo
/ē/	tea	rey
/ī/	tie	baile
/ō/	toe	dos
/ū/	use	ayuder
/aw/	paw	_____
/oy/	boy	soy
/ow/	cow	causa
/o͝o/	book	_____
/o͞o/	too	unos
/ə/	sofa	_____

Consonant Differences

Spanish has fewer consonant sounds than English does. As indicated in Table XXIV, Spanish has no /v/ as in **violin**, /z/ as in **zebra**, /sh/ as in **shoe**, /ŋ/ as in **wing**, /hw/ as in **where**, or /zh/ sound as in **azure**. However, Spanish has a trilled **r** sound as in **perro** that is not present in English.

Even when the two languages share consonant sounds, additional interference in understanding is caused by the way some of the phonemes are articulated. For example, when Spanish speakers pronounce /p/ before stressed vowels, it is perceived as a /b/ by English speakers so that **pill** sounds like **bill**. In addition, **d** and **p** are not articulated with as much force in Spanish as they are in English.

TABLE XXIV

English and Spanish Consonant Sounds

English		Spanish
/b/	bat	bajo
/d/	dog	doy
/f/	fan	fama
/g/	gun	gota
/h/	hand	julio
/j/	joy	———
/k/	cat	casa, que
/l/	line	la
/m/	man	mucho
/n/	nine	nada
/p/	pot	poco
/r/	rug	aro
/s/	sand	sei
/t/	top	tal
/v/	van	———
/w/	watch	huevo
/y/	young	yo
/z/	zebra	———
/ch/	cheese	mucho
/ŋ/	ring	———
/sh/	ship	———
/th/	thin	zumo (not pronounced in some dialects)
/th/	then	madre, nada
/hw/	when	———
/zh/	garage	———
/rr/	———	carro

Differences in Distribution

There are also differences in distribution. Spanish consonants have a much more restricted placement in words. Only /d/, /s/, /n/, /r/, and /l/ occur in final position. Most English consonants can occur in beginning, medial, or final positions. Exceptions include /h/ (**hat**), /w/ (**we**), /y/ (**you**), which are only found in initial position. (The **h** and **w** at the end of **oh** and **law** are letters used to help spell /ō/ and /aw/ and do not represent consonant sounds. The **y** at the end of **try** and **city** represents vowel sounds and does not function in those words as a consonant.) On the other hand, the English consonants /ŋ/ (**ring**) and /zh/ (**beige**) can only occur in final position.

Clusters

Both Spanish and English have consonants known as clusters or blends. In general, Spanish clusters occur only in initial position. Although there are some clusters in English that occur only in initial **gr-graph, bl-blue**) or final position (**nd-hand, nt-bent**), there are a few clusters that can be found in both initial and final position (**st-stop, st-best, sk-skate, sk-ask**).

POTENTIAL PROBLEM AREAS

Because of differences in number of speech sounds, exact manner of articulation, and distribution of speech sounds, Spanish-speaking children may have difficulty perceiving and pronouncing some English sounds. Some potential problems for native speakers of Spanish learning English are listed below. The list has been adapted from O'Brien (1973).

Consonants

/b/ The sound /b/ may be pronounced /p/ so that **bat** becomes **pat** and **cub** becomes **cup.**

/d/ The sound /d/ may be pronounced or sound like /t/ so that **dot** becomes **tot** and **bead** becomes **beat.**

/f/ The sound /f/ does not occur in final position in Spanish. The sound /f/ may be omitted at the end of a word so that **if** is pronounced **ih.**

/g/ Since this sound only occurs in initial position in Spanish, it may be omitted or replaced by /k/ at the end of a word so that **bag** becomes **bah** or **back.**

/j/ There is no /j/ sound in Spanish. May be pronounced or perceived as /y/ so that **Jello**® becomes **yellow.**

/k/ May be omitted at the end of a word so that **pick** becomes **pih.**

/p/ The sound /p/ spoken before a stressed vowel may be perceived as /b/ by speakers of English. Final /p/ occurs infrequently. May be confused with /b/ so that **cup** is pronounced as **cub.**

/l/ May be omitted at the end of a word so that **pole** becomes **poe.**

/m/ Final /m/ occurs infrequently. May be pronounced or perceived as /n/ so that **sum** becomes **sun.**

/ŋ/ There is no /ŋ/ sound in Spanish. May be pronounced as /n/ so that **sing** becomes **sin.**

/r/ May be trilled so that **pair** sounds like **pairirr.**

/t/ Final /t/, which occurs infrequently in Spanish, may be omitted so that **tent** becomes **ten.**

/ch/ May be pronounced or perceived as /sh/ so that **choose** becomes **shoes.**

/sh/ There is no /sh/ sound in Spanish. May be pronounced or perceived as /ch/ so that **shop** is pronounced as **chop.**

/th/ Voiceless **th** is often pronounced as **d, t,** or **s** by many speakers of Spanish so that **thing** becomes **ding, ting,** or **sing.**

/v/ The sound /v/ might be pronounced as /b/ so that **volt** is pronounced as **bolt.**

/y/ May be pronounced as /j/ so that **yo-yo** becomes **jo-jo.**

/z/ May be omitted at the end of a word so that **goes** becomes **go.**

/sk/, /sp/, /st/ Clusters in Spanish may begin with /e/ but not /s/. Because Spanish has words that begin with /esk/, /esp/, and /est/ but not /sk/, /sp/, or /st/, **speak** becomes **espeak, stair** becomes **estair,** and **skate** becomes **eskate.**

Vowels

/a/ There is no short **a** in Spanish. Short **a** is often pronounced as a short **e.** The word **adverb** may be pronounced as **edverb.**

/e/ Short **e** is often pronounced as short **a.** The word **let** might be pronounced **lat.**

/i/ There is no short **i** in Spanish. Short **i** is often substituted for long **e** and vice versa. **Sit** is pronounced as **seat,** and **beat** is pronounced as **bit.**

/u/ Short **u** is often pronounced as a short **o.** The word **hut** may be pronounced as **hot.**

/aw/ There is no /aw/ **(paw)** sound in Spanish. Students may substitute a short **o** sound for **aw. Paw** might be pronounced as **pah.**

/o͞o/ There is no /o͞o/ (book) sound in Spanish. Short **oo** is often pronounced like long **oo. Would** is pronounced **woold.**

/ə/ There is no schwa in Spanish. Schwa may be pronounced as **ah. Sofa** might be pronounced as **sofah.**

/r/ The Spanish **rr** is trilled so students may have difficulty with **r** vowels such as **sir** and **turn.**

TEACHING PHONIC ELEMENTS

Students won't be able to learn a letter-sound relationship if they can't perceive the sound being taught or if they confuse it with another sound. Students will need special help when dealing with a sound that doesn't occur in their native tongue. Before introducing sound elements that might pose problems, develop necessary auditory discrimination and perception by using activities similar to those described below, which are designed to prepare the student for the **sh** = /sh/ correspondence.

Activity 1

Have students answer questions similar to the following:

1. (Holding up a picture of sheep) Are these seep or sheep?
2. (Holding up a saw) Is this a saw or a shawl?
3. (Pointing to a seat) Is this a seat or a sheet?
4. (Pointing to a shelf) Is this a self or a shelf?
5. (Holding up a sea shell) Is this a sell or a shell?
6. (Holding up a picture of a ship) Is this a sip or a ship?
7. (Holding up a sock) Is this a sock or a shock?
8. (Holding up a shoe) Is this a sue or a shoe?
9. (Holding up a picture of the sun) Is this the sun or the shun?
10. (Shaking your hand) Am I saking or shaking my hand?

Activity 2

Read the following word pairs to students. Have them raise one hand if the words are different and two if they are the same.

sheep — sheep
sip — ship
see — she
sue — shoe
so — so
sack — shack
so — show
sale — shale
same — shame
sun — sun

Activity 3

Have students answer questions similar to the following:
1. (Holding up a shoe) Is this a shoe or a chew?
2. (Pointing to your chin) Is this a chin or a shin?
3. (Pointing to a chair) Is this a chair or a share?
4. (Holding up a picture of sheep) Is this a cheap or a sheep?
5. (Holding up a picture of a ship) Is this a chip or a ship?
6. (Holding up a sheet) Is this a cheat or a sheet?
7. (Holding up a potato chip) Is this a potato chip or a potato ship?
8. (Holding up a picture of cheese) Is this cheese or she's?
9. (Holding up a pair of shoes) Are these choose or shoes?
10. (Holding up a picture of a baby chick) Is this a chick or a shick?

Activity 4

Read the following word pairs to students. Have them raise one hand if the two words are different and two if they are the same.

choose — shoes
chip — chip
chop — shop
chew — shoe
share — share
cheap — sheep
chin — shin
cheat — sheet
shore — shore
cheer — sheer

Activity 5

Have students sort objects by sound, putting each in the /ch/ (**chair**), /sh/ (**shoes**), or /s/ (**saw**) box depending upon whether the object begins with /ch/, /sh/, or /s/. Objects might include toy shoes, chalk, a toy saw, a saddle, salt, sand, cut-out numeral **six**, cut-out numeral **seven,** a shell, soap, a toy chicken, a toy sheep, toy church, a drawing of the sun, a shirt, a toy ship, or a toy shovel. Before beginning the activity, discuss the names of all the objects and their functions if students are unfamiliar with them.

Activity 6

Present oral sentences in which students pick the word that best fits the sense of the sentence.

1. I saw a (chip, ship) heading for the dock.
2. The new (choose, shoes) fit just right.
3. He has a small beard on his (chin, shin).
4. Which book did you (choose, shoes)?
5. We looked at the puppies in the pet (chop, shop).
6. We will (cheer, sheer) for our school's team.
7. You must (chew, shoe) your food carefully.
8. Draw a picture of that (cheat, sheet) of paper.
9. They are rowing the boat to (chore, shore).
10. Sit in this (chair, share).

Activity 7

Have students cut out or draw pictures of objects that begin like /sh/.

In classroom discussions when using words that begin with /sh/ or other easily confused sounds, try to use the words in context so that students have an additional clue to the word you are using. Word lists for creating additional auditory discrimination exercises of sounds likely to be confused by Spanish speakers are printed at the end of this chapter.

EMPHASIS ON UNDERSTANDING

Resist the temptation to equate reading and speech. Some students will still be grappling with English pronunciation long after they have mastered a fairly respectable recognition vocabulary. In reading, the key is understanding not pronunciation. If a student reads "Yo got a new pair of choose," but understands that Joe got new footwear, then the student is reading accurately. The mispronunciation of **Joe** and **shoes** is a language learning or articulation rather than a reading problem.

TRANSITIONAL PROGRAMS

Students who are already literate in their native tongue learn to read in English fairly rapidly. However, they will most likely need extra help in English phonics and English vocabulary. Programs designed to provide for the special needs of these youngsters are now beginning to appear. *The Houghton Mifflin Transition* (Barrera & Crawford, 1987), for instance, is a three-book series designed to help youngsters move into the publisher's English reading series.

Emphasis is placed on developing vocabulary, concepts, and phonics. Students may start off in Level 1, which covers first-grade reading, Level 2, which covers second-grade reading, or Level 3, which covers third-grade reading. The program is structured so that students can move rapidly through each level. The first ten pages of each workbook review phonics elements previously introduced.

WORD LISTS FOR EASILY CONFUSED SOUNDS

Listed below are word pairs that might be used to build auditory discrimination of sounds that Spanish-speaking youngsters are likely to find difficult.

/ē/	and	/i/		/e/	and	/ā/
eat		it		bet		bait
each		itch		get		gate
beat		bit		let		late
deep		dip		men		main
heat		hit		met		mate
bead		bid		pen		pain
bean		bin		red		raid
heal		hill		sell		sail
meat		mitt		tell		tail
				wet		wait

/a/	and	/o/		/o͞o/	and	/o͝o/
ax		ox		fool		full
bag		bog		Luke		look
cab		cob		pool		pull
cat		cot		suit		soot
hat		hot		shoed		should
map		mop				
pat		pot				
sack		sock				
rat		rot				

/b/	and	/p/
cab		cap
cub		cup
cob		cop
mob		mop
rib		rip
robe		rope
slab		slap
sub		sup
tab		tap
bob		bop

/b/	and	/v/
boat		vote
ban		van
banish		vanish
bat		vat
bent		vent
berry		very
best		vest
bet		vet
ballet		vallet
ballad		valid

/g/	and	/k/
pig		pick
peg		peck
bag		back
tag		tack
bug		buck
chug		chuck
clog		clock
dug		duck
rag		rack

/j/	and	/y/
Jack		yak
jam		yam
jell		yell
jeer		year
jet		yet
jello		yellow
Jess		yes
jo-jo		yo-yo

/m/	and	/n/
sum		sun
am		an
beam		bean
cam		can
came		cane
comb		cone
dime		dine
game		gain
gum		gun
hem		hen

/n/	and	/ŋ/
sin		sing
thin		thing
fan		fang
kin		king
pan		pang
ran		rang
stun		stung
win		wing
ban		bang
sun		sung

CHAPTER XI

MATERIALS FOR REINFORCING
WORD ATTACK SKILLS

THERE IS NO lack of material for practicing word attack skills. Kits, workbooks, sets of duplicating masters, games, and computer software abound, especially in the area of phonics. Although fairly lengthy, the listing of materials in this chapter is not exhaustive. A complete listing of all word attack materials is beyond the scope of this text. Moreover, the inclusion of material in this chapter should not be taken as a recommendation. Teachers should examine all materials in the light of their approach to the teaching of reading and in view of the particular needs of their students.

In general, materials that provide opportunities to practice skills in context are better than those that do not. Supplementary word attack materials should also be used selectively. For example, don't assign each child every page of a workbook. Assign only those pages that contain exercises which provide needed reinforcement. If your second graders have mastered initial consonants, don't waste their time by having them complete exercises that review initial consonants, even though these are typically found in second-grade phonics worktexts.

Also cast a critical eye on exercises. Remember the purpose of teaching word attack skills is to make students skillful decoders. If an exercise doesn't, in some way, help children to achieve that goal, then by all means skip it.

Descriptions of workbooks, computer software, kits, games and other materials that might be used to reinforce word attack skills are contained on the following pages. Publishers' addresses are listed at the back of the book.

WORKBOOKS

The Barnell Loft 500. Barnell Loft.
  Each text in this five-book series develops 100 sight words. Elementary.

Basic Skills Phonics Program. Frank Schaffer.
  A set of twelve books reinforces basic phonics skills. Emphasis is on interesting formats. Elementary.

Developing Dictionary Skills. Good Apple.
  Duplicating masters reinforce key dictionary skills. Elementary and middle school.

Discovering Phonics We Use. Riverside.
  This eight-book program begins with readiness and extends up through skills typically presented in sixth grade. Structural and morphemic analysis, dictionary, and word meaning skills are presented along with phonic activities. Elementary.

Focus on Phonics. New Readers Press.
  This four-book series covers basic phonics skills. The series may be used independently or in conjunction with *The Laubach Way to Reading,* an adult literacy series. Secondary and adult.

Frisky Phonics I, II. Good Apple.
  Dogs are used to make phonics exercises more interesting in these two 152-page workbooks. Primary.

The Ginn Word Enrichment Program. Ginn.
  Although the focus of this primary program is on phonics, vocabulary and word analysis skills are also developed. Beginning with Book B, this seven-book program presents words in patterns. Elementary.

Homonym Puzzles. Curriculum Associates.
  Thirty puzzles in duplicating master format provide practice with 350 homonyms. Elementary.

Language Arts Phonics. Scholastic.
  This three-book series relates phonics to writing instruction. Primary.

Megawords. Educators Publishing Service.
  This eight-book series provides practice in dealing with multisyllabic words in reading and spelling. Elementary and secondary.

Merrill Phonics: Skilltext Series. Merrill.
  This five-book series begins with readiness skills and ends with dictionary skills. Additional reinforcement exercises for the first three

levels are presented on software designed to be run on the Apple. Elementary.

Modern Curriculum Press Phonics Workbooks. Modern Curriculum Press.

This six-book series covers basic word attack skills. Elementary.

Mott Basic Language Skills Program. Allied Education Council.

The beginning books in this series present a phonics program for adults. Real photos instead of illustrations are used in exercises to give the texts a mature format. Workbooks are available in regular and semi-programmed series. Secondary and adult.

My Short Book. My Long Book. I Can Write Book. Curriculum Associates.

In this three-book series, short, long, and other vowels are introduced via story characters and short poems. Elementary.

New Phonics and Word Analysis Skills. Continental.

A variety of exercises are designed to reinforce phonics and other word attack skills typically taught in grades 1-6. Series is available in 72-page workbooks, in sets of duplicating masters, or blackline masters. Masters are only published for grades 1-4. Elementary.

A New Time for Phonics. McGraw-Hill.

Each book in this five-book series develops one major aspect of phonics: consonants, short vowels, long vowels, consonant pairs, patterns, and syllables. Elementary.

Phonics. Milliken.

Four 64-page books present basic phonics skills. Elementary.

Phonics Fun. Continental.

This three-book primary series is available in duplicating or blackline masters. Presents cut-and-paste activities designed to reinforce phonics skills. Primary.

Phonics Mastery. Harcourt.

Seven sets of duplicating masters present basic phonics skills. Set 6 includes sixty-four masters; the other sets contain thirty-two. Elementary.

Phonics Skills. Essential Learning.

Basic phonics skills are presented in a series of five 8¼″ × 5¼″ workbooks. Students may find the small size appealing. Elementary.

Phonics Skills. Milliken.

Eight sets of duplicating masters reinforce basic phonics skills. Each set contains twenty masters. Elementary.

Power Words Program. Steck-Vaughn.

This four-book series introduces and reinforces 202 high frequency words. Practice exercises include cloze-type activities, a number of games, and reading selections. Elementary.

Primary Phonics. Educators Publishing Service.

Although most phonics series are designed for average youngsters, this series would be especially appropriate for slower youngsters. The series, which is meant for students in kindergarten through grade four, consists of six 80-page workbooks accompanied by five series of ten illustrated 16-page storybooks. The series' varied exercises stress meaning. In addition, many of the exercises involve coloring, which is a highly motivating activity for youngsters. Elementary.

Random House Phonics. Random House.

This three-book series covers basic phonics skills and fits in with a patterned or linguistic approach. Elementary.

Reach for Reading. Modern Curriculum Press.

This single workbook presents readiness and basic phonics skills. Designed for older students, the workbook includes exercises using everyday reading materials and comic-strip formats. Secondary.

The Schmeller Reading Program. Instructional Sequence. EMC.

A set of eighteen workbooks provides thorough, structured coverage of phonics and syllabication skills. Readers, flashcards, and wall-charts are also available. Recommended for LD and EMR students. Elementary.

Schmeller Reader Program. S. T.A.R. T. EMC.

This six-book series presents beginning phonics skills. Recommended for LD and EMR students. Elementary.

Schoolhouse Press Phonics Program. Schoolhouse.

This three-level program presents basic word attack skills. Designed to provide plenty of practice, each book contains 272 pages. Blackline assessment masters are contained in the teacher's edition. Elementary.

Sounds We Use. Hayes.

Three 64-page workbooks present basic phonics skills.

Steck-Vaughn Phonics. Steck-Vaughn.

This four-book series contains a variety of reinforcement exercises including a limited number of brief reading selections in levels B, C, and D but not A. Books decrease in length as they reach into higher levels. Book A has 188 pages; Book B has 140; C and D have only 108. The series is generously illustrated with four-color photos and drawings. Elementary.

Step Up. Educators Publishing Service.

This four-book series of 20 to 25-page booklets is designed for young remedial pupils. The sequence of skills follows that of the Gillingham approach. Elementary.

Vocabulary Skills. Scholastic.

This six-book series provides instruction and practice with word families, affixes, root words, and context. Elementary.

Vowel Fun. Good Apple.

Mazes, puzzles, and cut-and-paste activities reinforce knowledge of vowel correspondences. Primary.

A Word Recognition Program. Barnell Loft.

This five-level program ranges from readiness through advanced word attack skills. Elementary.

COMPUTER SOFTWARE

Although much maligned, computer software has shown a steady improvement over the past few years. The most important development is the addition of sound to programs so that students can both see a letter and hear the sound that the letter represents. The sound in some programs has a robot-like quality while that in other programs is more human. In general, digitized speech is superior to synthesized speech. You may want to listen to phonics programs that have a speech component before making a purchase.

Apart from the sound, the major advantage of computer software is that it provides endless, patient reinforcement for those youngsters who need a lot of practice. The computer is also nonjudgmental and provides immediate knowledge of results, which is a powerful reinforcer.

Basic Phonics. Curriculum Associates.

Designed for special needs students, this eight-disk series presents and reinforces skills ranging from beginning consonants to short and long vowel review. Apple. 64K. Elementary.

Criterion Mastery Series. Queue.

Individual programs provide practice in a variety of word attack skills ranging from working with initial consonants to working with affixes. Apple. Elementary.

Compound Words and Contractions. Hartley.

This three-disk series presents and provides practice with compound words and contractions. Additional compounds and contractions may be added. Apple. Elementary.

Consonants and Vowels. Intellectual Software. Queue.

This five-disk series presents both pictorial and verbal contextual exercises.

Context Clues Hidden Treasure. Learning Well.

Students practice using context clues within the framework of a seeking treasure game. Can be played alone or with a partner. Teacher can enter own exercises. Can also view student's scores, print out scores, and extend game so that it becomes more challenging. Comes in two levels: red and blue. Red has a 2.0-3.5 readability. Blue has a 3.5-5.0 readability. Apple. Elementary.

First-Letter Fun. MECC.

Involves matching letters with pictures whose names start with certain sounds. Letters and illustrations are presented within the context of interesting scenes: a farm, circus, magic act, and park. Letters can be shown in upper or lower case. Requires minimal use of keystrokes to accommodate students with special needs. Apple. Primary.

Hint and Hunt I and II, *Construct-A-Word* I and II, *Syllasearch* I, II, III, and IV. DLM.

In the *Hint* portion of *Hint and Hunt,* words — both real and nonsense — are pronounced and the student chooses the vowel letter that spells the spoken sound. In *Hunt,* the student plays a Pacman-type game with words containing the phonic elements that have been introduced. *Construct a Word* continues where *Hint and Hunt* leaves off. More complex single-syllable words are presented. Emphasis is on building words by combining beginnings and endings. In *Syllasearch,* students analyze and manipulate multisyllabic words of gradually increasing difficulty. Disks are accompanied by blackline masters, a teacher's guide, and pre and posttests. Apple. Uses synthesized speech. Requires Echo or Cricket (Apple IIc) voice synthesizer. Elementary and secondary remedial.

The Montana Reading Program: Learning Sight Words. Program Design International.

Reinforces the 220 sight words from the Dolch list. Presents each sight word in a sentence. The sight word fades away and the child is asked to type the missing word in a box that has a configuration that matches that of the sight word. If the student makes a mistake, an outline of the word is supplied. Words are presented in five levels. Student is given a pretest to determine appropriate starting level. Set of sight word cards accompany the software. The manual contains suggestions for conducting practice activities with the cards. Apple, Atari, Commodore. Elementary.

Phonics Prime Time: Initial Consonants. MECC.

Uses two games to present initial consonants. The first game involves matching a letter to a picture whose name starts with that letter. The second involves using knowledge of consonants to choose a word and fill in the blank in an incomplete sentence. The incomplete sentence is composed of sight words. Requires minimal use of keystrokes to accommodate special needs students. Apple. Primary.

Phonics Prime Time: Final Consonants. MECC.

Uses two games to reinforce final consonants. Requires minimal use of keystrokes to accommodate special needs students. Apple. Elementary.

Phonics Prime Time: Blends and Digraphs. MECC.

Uses shopping trips to reinforce consonant clusters and digraphs. Requires minimal use of keystrokes to accommodate special needs students. Apple. Primary.

Phonics Prime Time: Vowels I and Vowels II. MECC.

Vowels I uses carnival games to reinforce knowledge of long and short vowel correspondences. *Vowels II* reinforces **r** vowels, vowel digraphs, and other vowels. Requires minimal use of keystrokes to accommodate special needs students. Apple. Primary.

Reader Rabbit and the Fabulous Word Factory. Learning Company. Society for Visual Education.

Students are introduced to 200 three-letter words in a fun activity. Apple, Commodore, IBM. Primary.

Roots/Affixes. Hartley.

This two-disk set provides instruction and practice with roots and affixes. Lessons are inductive and include context. If a student has difficulty with an item, she has the option of asking for a hint or an explanation. Student's score is given upon completion of a series of lessons. Teachers can change lessons by adding, deleting, or changing existing frames. Lessons may also be printed. Apple. Elementary.

Roots and Affixes. Hartley.

This two-disk program presents twenty-one lessons ranging from simple roots and affixes to more complex ones. Apple. Elementary.

Sight Words. Curriculum Associates.

The first diskette in this two-diskette series presents sight words on a preprimer, primer, and first-grade level. The second diskette presents words on the first- and second-grade levels. Apple. Elementary.

The Smart Alex Phonics Program. Smart Alex Press.

Containing 112 lessons and more than 1,100 teaching activities, Alex is an extensive phonics program. Through the use of a specially designed interface, the program synchronizes tutorial lessons on pre-recorded cassette tapes with a visual display presented on a computer screen. Unlike the voice in many computer programs, Alex's voice is clear and undistorted. Provision is also made for dialect variation so students won't be confused when the way the word is pronounced on the tape differs somewhat from the way they say it. The program presents consonants, clusters, long, short, other vowels, and schwa. Diagnostic tests are included. Alex is comprised of twenty-two tapes and four diskettes. Apple, Commodore 64, IBM PC, and TRS80. Elementary.

Snoopy's Reading Machine. Random.

Using the word families **-at, -et, -ig, -op, -ug,** students create words and see the words depicted on the screen. Apple, Commodore 64. Primary.

Sound Ideas. Houghton Mifflin.

Includes three components: *Consonants, Vowels,* and *Word Attack. Consonants* presents seventeen consonants and three digraphs. *Vowels* presents the short vowels and vowel sounds represented by the letter **y.** *Word Attack* reinforces consonant clusters and digraphs, vowel digraphs, and sentence context. Accompanying workbooks are an important part of the program. Uses synthesized speech. Apple. Requires Echo and/or Cricket (Apple IIc) speech synthesizer. Elementary.

Stickybear ABC. Weekly Reader.

In this award-winning program, students press a key and objects appear whose names begin with the sound represented by the letter pushed. Apple. Primary.

SUPERLEAD. LEAD Educational Resources.

SUPERLEAD is a computerized version of *LEAD,* an acronym for *Logical Encoding and Decoding. SUPERLEAD* is a tightly structured comprehensive program that presents all the sounds of English, the most frequent spellings of these sounds, and the Dolch words. This six-disk program incorporates a careful introduction of phonic elements and a variety of reinforcement opportunities including games. This program is accompanied by a teacher's guide. Each disk has pre and posttests. Apple. Elementary and secondary remedial.

Talking Textwriter. Scholastic.

This word processing program is accompanied by speech so that the words the students type in are sounded out by a speech synthesizer. This means that students can get help with a word that they can't read. When the student types in an unknown word, the computer will "read" it. Apple. Uses synthesized speech. Requires Echo and/or Echo b. Elementary.

Using Phonics in Context. Educational Activities.

This five-diskette program combines practice in phonics and comprehension so that students use their decoding skills in a realistic way. The program includes a pretest and a management system. Apple. Upper elementary remedial and secondary remedial.

Vocabulary-Dolch. Hartley.

Sight words are presented orally through a tape recorder attached to the computer via a connection known as the Cassette Control Device (CCD). A record is kept of students' responses. Apple. Requires a CCD and tape recorder. Elementary.

Vowels Tutorial. Hartley.

Spoken instruction is provided by a CCD, which is a device that attaches a tape recorder to the computer. Program branches when student makes an error. A record is kept of errors. Apple. Requires CCD and tape recorder. Elementary.

Word Families I. Hartley.

Provides practice with consonant substitution by having students replace single letters to form new words. Teacher may add words and letters. Apple, IBM. Elementary.

Word Families II. Hartley.

Students form new words by substituting consonant combinations. Teacher may change any of the program's sixteen lessons. Apple, IBM. Elementary.

Word Memory Programs. Instructional/Communications.

Provides practice with sight vocabulary. Comes in several versions. Each version presents words drawn from a specific major basal. Contains a management program. Apple. Primary.

Word Munchers. MECC.

Uses a game format to reinforce knowledge of long and short vowel correspondences. Apple. Primary.

Word Parts. Teacher Support Software.

Students learn phonograms and letter clusters in the context of an adventure. *Word Parts* comes in three levels for grades 1 and 2, 3 and

4 and 5 and 6. There are five disks on each level. Apple. Elementary.

Words at Work: Compound It! MECC.

Provides practice with compound words. Apple. Upper elementary.

Words at Work: Suffix Sense. MECC.

Provides practice with sixteen suffixes. Apple. Upper elementary.

Working with Words. Intellectual Software. Queue.

Exercises combine use of context with use of phonics skills. Apple. Elementary.

KITS, GAMES, AND OTHER MATERIALS

AIMS. Continental.

A series of three kits provides illustrated folders and a variety of manipulative devices for reinforcing phonics skills. Should be especially useful for special needs students. Primary.

Brigance Prescriptive Word Analysis: Strategies and Practice, Volumes I and II. Curriculum Associates.

Volume I contains teaching suggestions and practice activities for introducing and reinforcing consonant and short and long vowel correspondences. *Volume II* contains suggestions and materials for introducing and reinforcing other vowels, vowel digraphs, multisyllabic words, and affixes.

Consonant Sounds/A Self-Instructional Modalities Approach, Vowel Sounds/A Self-Instructional Modalities Approach. Media Materials.

Students use visual, auditory, and kinesthetic modalities to learn consonant and vowel sounds. Each kit contains ten audio cassettes, five manipulatives, and ten packs of 72 response sheets.

Decoding Keys for Reading Success. Walker.

Kits come in three levels: primary, intermediate, and advanced. Each kit contains 1800 words that develop from 115 to 127 sound clusters or pronounceable units (**ab, an, ug**). Each sound cluster is presented in from fourteen to seventeen words. Elementary and secondary.

Developing A Basic Sight Vocabulary. Barnell Loft.

Wall charts, workbooks, readers, and sentence and word cards are used to present and reinforce 187 sight words. Elementary.

Developing Structural Analysis Kits. System 80. Educational Technology.

A series of three kits reinforces contractions, affixes, root words, and syllabication. A synchronized sound-sight presentation is made via a special viewing-listening device.

Eye-Ear-Hand Phonics. Educational Activities.

Stories on audio cassettes are used to present basic elements of phonics. Accompanying exercises are contained in workbooks or ditto masters. Three separate packages present initial consonants, consonant digraphs and blends, and long and short vowels. Elementary.

Glass Analysis for Decoding Only. Walker.

Presents 119 pronounceable letter clusters in 2,300 words. Kit contains packs of cards and 32-page practice books. Elementary and secondary remedial.

Improving Phonics Skills: System 80. Educational Technology.

A series of six kits reinforces basic phonics skills. A synchronized sound-sight presentation is made via a special viewing-listening device. Elementary.

Learning Letter Sounds. System 80. Educational Technology.

A series of six kits presents consonants, consonant clusters, and phonograms. A synchronized sound-sight presentation is made via a special viewing-listening device.

Phonovisual. Phonovisual.

The Phonovisual method advocates teaching phonics as a separate subject for fifteen to thirty minutes a day. Materials include wall-charts, workbooks, duplicating masters, a variety of games, film-strips, and diagnostic tests. Elementary.

Picture Flash Words. Media Materials.

Each of these 118 flash cards has a sight word and picture on the front side and the word alone on the reverse side. Elementary.

Reading Skills Kit. Visual, Auditory, and Kinesthetic Activities. Zaner-Bloser.

Develops sight words, auditory discrimination, and beginning sounds. Emphasis is on using child's strongest modality. Each skill has activities that are primarily visual, auditory, or kinesthetic. Kit includes a teacher's guide, alphabet and word cards, posters, pupil record, spinner, and blackline masters. Readiness.

Reading Words in Context. System 80. Educational Technology.

A series of seventeen kits develops 680 high-frequency words. A synchronized sound-sight presentation is made via a special viewing-listening device. Elementary.

Road Race. Curriculum Associates.

This board game provides practice with consonants, consonant combinations, and phonograms. Elementary.

Step Up to Reading Success. Educational Activities.

This kit contains bulletin board material, flash cards, and a variety of games for reinforcing readiness skills, sight vocabulary, and a variety of phonics skills. Elementary.

Structural Skill Quizmo. Media Materials.

In a game with a lotto format, students practice recognizing affixes and roots. Middle school.

TV Tutor Sight Words 1 and *2.* New Readers Press.

Each tape presents thirty high-frequency words in ten lessons. Tapes are accompanied by worksheets. Secondary and adult.

You Can Read — Phonetic Drill Cards. Media Materials.

This set of twenty-three hinged cards, by making use of word families and consonants and consonant combinations, can be used to build 345 words.

CHILDREN'S BOOKS THAT CAN BE USED TO REINFORCE WORD ATTACK SKILLS

Berenstain, Stan & Jan. *The Bears' Vacation.* New York: Random, 1968.
Compound words, multisyllabic words.

Berenstain, Stan & Jan. *C Is for Clown.* New York: Random, 1972.
Sight words, c = /k/ sound, cl, cr.

Cerf, Bennett. *Cerf's Book of Riddles.* New York: Random, 1960.
Sight words, easy multisyllabic words.

Eastman, P.D. *Are You My Mother?* New York: Random, 1960.
Sight words, basic phonics.

Eastman, P.D. *Sam and the Firefly.* New York: Random, 1958.
Sight words, basic phonics.

Greene, Carol. *Snow Joe.* Chicago: Children's Press, 1982.
Long o.

Hillert, Margaret. *Circus Fun.* Cleveland: Modern Curriculum Press, 1969.
Sight words, color words.

Hillert Margaret. *The Three Goats.* Chicago: Follett, 1963.
Sight words, color words.

Johnson, Mildred. *Wait, Skates.* Chicago: Children's Press, 1983.
Sight words, long a.

Lesieg, Theodore. *Ten Apples up on Top.* New York: Random, 1961.
Sight words, number words, short o.

Lopshire, R. *Put Me in the Zoo*. New York: Random, 1960.
   Sight words, various spellings of long **oo** words.
Moncure, Jane. *Word Bird Makes Words with Cat*. Elgin, IL: The Child's
   World, 1984.
   Sight words, short **a** words.
Moncure, Jane. *Word Bird Makes Words with Dog*. Elgin, IL: The Child's
   World, 1984.
   Sight words, short **o** words.
Moncure, Jane. *Word Bird Makes Words with Hen*. Elgin, IL: The Child's
   World, 1984.
   Sight words, short **e** words.
Petrie, Catherine. *Sandbox Betty*. Chicago: Children's Press, 1982.
   The **al** spelling of /aw/ and other vowel patterns.
Rockwell, A. *Big Bad Goat*. New York: E.P. Dutton, 1982.
   Sight words, **sc, str, st, sh, ch, fl.**
Sadler, M. *The Very Bad Bunny*. New York: Random, 1984.
   Compound words, multisyllabic words.
Dr. Suess. *The Cat in the Hat Comes Back*. New York: Random, 1958.
   Compound words, basic phonics.
Dr. Suess. *The Foot Book*. New York: Random, 1968.
   Sight words, **ee** spelling of long **e.**
Wolcote, P. *The Cake Story*. Reading, MA: Addison-Wesley, 1974.
   Long **a** words.

CHAPTER XII

EVALUATION OF WORD ATTACK SKILLS

THE INFORMAL READING INVENTORY

THE BEST WAY to test students' ability to decode words is to administer an informal reading inventory and to analyze the results. The first portion of the inventory is a word recognition in isolation test. Students are asked to read graded lists of words ranging from a preprimer to an eighth or high school level. The examiner writes down the student's incorrect responses and then analyzes these in terms of elements known and unknown. A careful analysis should yield information about a student's sight vocabulary, phonics skills, and ability to handle multisyllabic words.

The second part of an informal reading inventory consists of reading graded oral and silent passages. By analyzing errors, the tester can obtain useful information about students' word attack skills in context. See *Informal Reading Inventories* (Johnson, Kress, Pikulski, 1987) for a full explanation of the administration and interpretation of reading inventories.

COMMERCIALLY PRODUCED PHONICS TESTS

There are a number of commercially produced tests of phonics. Some are parts of batteries that include tests of comprehension. Others are devoted solely to word attack skills. Some can be given in groups. Others must be administered individually.

Group Phonics Tests

Group tests of phonics suffer from a number of deficiencies. Many formats used to evaluate phonics knowledge actually test spelling. If the tester says a word and the student responds by writing the consonant that the word begins with or the letters that represent the vowel sound heard in the middle of the word, then this is really a test of spelling. The results can be indicative of decoding knowledge. However, the tester needs to keep in mind that spelling tends to be more difficult than reading so the inability to spell a word doesn't mean the student can't read it. Other group tests may ask the student to circle the letter that the name of an accompanying picture begins with or that represents the first sound of a word that the teacher says. This, too, is a spelling task. However, the student is aided by having possible answers narrowed down to three or four choices.

Some group phonics tests ask the student to indicate whether a vowel is **long** or **short.** Students may be able to read words containing long or short vowels but may not be able to say whether they are long or short.

One format, which is used in some standardized tests, requires students to choose from four alternatives the one that has the same sound as that underlined in the key word. For example, students might be asked to choose the word that has the same vowel sound as **go.** The choices might be **chow, bureau, ton,** and **true.** In a tryout of this type of format with elementary school youngsters, the author found that many youngsters who could read the target items in other formats had difficulty with this task. This type of format seemed more difficult than the actual task of reading.

The best format for testing decoding skills in a group situation seems to be one that involves using the decoding skill to read real words. One possible format is to choose from three or four illustrations the one that best shows a printed word. For example, in testing the **oa** $= /\bar{o}/$ correspondence, the student would read the words **boat, coat,** and **goat** and choose the pictures that show these.

Farr and Carey (1986), discussing the different formats used on standardized tests, wondered what impact format has on skill measurement. They noted that different formats are used to test identical skills. They questioned whether diverse formats are really measuring the same thing.

Pikulski and Shanahan (1980) concluded that different formats produced different results, but were unable to say which format was best. Both Pikulski and Shanahan and Farr and Carey questioned the validity of testing phonics skills isolated from sentence or story context. Farr and Carey commented:

> In the case of a word recognition test, a prime validity concern is whether what it measures has any valid relationship to what readers do when they are actually reading. This concern focuses initially on

whether the various word recognition skills measured by different tests can actually be isolated so that the test takers' responses to items have any semblance to what is happening when they read for pleasure or for learning from content materials. (p. 79)

Individual Phonics Tests

Individual tests can be more valid than group tests. However, individual tests sometimes ask students to give the sound symbolized by a single letter. This works better with vowels than with consonants. Vowels can be pronounced in isolation; consonants are distorted if spoken without an accompanying vowel. If a teacher wants to determine whether students can decode initial consonants, then the teacher might ask the student to read words with those consonants. However, a wrong response might indicate difficulty with the middle or end of the word. To circumvent this problem, Ekwall (1988) proposed teaching the student common phonograms. The student would then add a consonant letter to the phonogram and read the word. For instance, after being taught **at,** the students would be shown **b + at** and would be asked to read the whole word. One problem with this procedure as implemented by Ekwall is that he used nonsense words (**sp + ut**).

The rationale for using nonsense words is that if real words are used and the student reads these accurately, this might mean that the student knew the words as sight words but might not be able to sound out words with similar elements. The major problem with nonsense words is that they short-circuit the decoding process. When sounding out unfamiliar words, students may try several pronunciations. They may reject nonwords, knowing that these can't be right, and try alternative pronunciations instead. However, if students are dealing with pseudowords, they don't have the opportunity to use this checking device. Moreover, there is some evidence that decoding nonsense words is more difficult than sounding out real words. Guthrie and Seifert (1977) found that of all the elements evaluated in an experimental phonics test, nonsense words were the most difficult.

OTHER WORD ATTACK SKILLS

As with phonics, the best way to evaluate word attack skills is in contextual situations. To assess students' ability to use affixes, combining forms, and roots, note how successful they are in dealing with these elements when they run across them in their reading. To evaluate ability to use dictionary skills, note how successful students are at looking up difficult words that they encounter in their reading. Were they able to locate the words? Were they able to obtain accurate pronunciations and appropriate definitions?

Note, too, how successful students are at completing workbook exercises devoted to reinforcing word attack skills. Many basal and supplementary series also have mastery tests that might be used to assess knowledge of word attack skills. State competency tests are another possible source of information about word attack proficiency. Some standardized reading tests also assess word attack skills.

WORD ATTACK TESTS

Perhaps because of the complexity of measuring phonics knowledge and other word attack skills, there are relatively few measures of decoding available. Listed below are some of the commercial tests that are available along with a brief description of each.

Individual Tests

Brigance Diagnostic Comprehensive Inventory of Basic Skills. Curriculum Associates.

Along with tests in twenty-three other areas, presents a section of seventeen tests in word analysis. Skills tested include auditory discrimination, consonants, vowels, suffixes, prefixes, and multisyllabic words. All of the tests except one on syllabication are designed for individual administration. Some thirteen reading programs were examined in order to determine the scope and sequence of skills tested.

A rationale for the tests is provided. Directions are clear and precise. Suggestions for additional tests or alternative testing procedures are frequently made.

Behavioral objectives are written for each test for the convenience of teachers who must compose instructional objectives for youngsters. Suggestions for instruction are contained in a separate manual.

Decoding Inventory. Kendall/Hunt.

Tests decoding skills on three levels: readiness, basic, and advanced. Covers major phonics skills and context, but uses nonsense words in most subtests and requires spelling rather than decoding in a number of subtests. Elementary.

Decoding Skills Test. York Press.

Consists of three subtests. Subtest I assesses reading vocabulary. Subtest II uses real and nonsense words to assess ability to decode phonic patterns in single and multisyllabic words. Subtest III uses oral paragraphs to assess the student's knowledge of the words and phonic patterns tested in Subtests I and II.

GFW Sound Symbols Test. American Guidance Service.

Seven areas are evaluated ranging from the ability to repeat nonsense words to the ability to spell nonsense words. The "Mimicry" subtest requires the youngster to repeat a nonsense word. "Recognition" involves matching a spoken word with a picture. "Analysis" requires orally producing the beginning, middle, or ending sound in a nonsense word. "Blending" evaluates the student's ability to blend a word spoken in parts. "Association" assesses the ability to associate nonletter symbols with nonsense words. "Reading" and "Spelling" test the ability to pronounce and spell nonsense words of gradually increasing difficulty. A carefully prepared answer sheet makes it possible to analyze errors and detect patterns. A performance profile makes it possible to compare scores among subtests. Since the *GWF Sound-Symbol Tests* are norm-referenced, students' scores can be compared with those of the norm group. Percentiles, stanines, grade equivalents, and standard scores are available.

Rosewell-Chall Diagnostic Reading Test of Word Analysis Skills, Revised and Extended, 1978. Essay.

This individually administered instrument provides a quick survey of word analysis skills of youngsters in grades 1 and 2 and remedial pupils reading on a first- or second-grade level. Assesses sight vocabulary, initial single consonants, consonant digraphs, and clusters, long and short vowels, vowel digraphs, dipthongs, and multisyllabic words. Supplementary tests include letter naming and spelling initial consonants and CVC words.

Sipay Word Analysis Tests (SWAT). Educators Publishing Service.

Composed of sixteen subtests and a survey test. Skills measured range from letter name and single letter sound symbol associations to visual blending of syllables. Uses real words to test skills. However, words were chosen that were not likely to be known as sight words. Many of these would be beyond the student's listening-speaking vocabulary, so in many instances the student would not be able to determine whether or not the word he or she pronounced is a real one. Since skills are tested in isolated words, there is no opportunity to see how the student uses them in context. It would be helpful to see how the student uses phonic and other word attack skills in conjunction with semantic and syntactic cues. The teacher could obtain this information by having the child read several appropriate passages after the *SWAT* has been administered. Also, more information on reliability, validity, and student tryouts should be supplied. Despite these weaknesses, the *SWAT* is carefully constructed, has excellent manuals, useful reporting forms, and is very thorough. Especially valuable are suggestions for analyzing the student's performance and testing in greater depth, if necessary.

Individual Diagnostic Reading Tests

Word attack skills are included in the batteries of most diagnostic reading tests. Briefly described below are the word attack skills included in the following three popular diagnostic batteries.

Diagnostic Reading Scales. McGraw-Hill.
Supplementary subtests assess basic phonics skills.
Durrell Analysis of Reading Difficulty. Psychological Corporation.
Initial and final consonants and clusters and consonant sounds in isolation are covered in two subtests.
Gates-McKillop-Horowitz Reading Diagnostic Tests. Teachers College Press.
Contains several subtests that measure consonant sounds in isolation, syllabication, blending of word parts, pronouncing nonsense words, and recognition of single vowels.

Group Tests

There is no question that individual tests are the best way to evaluate phonics skills. Both Sipay (1974) and Pikulski and Shannon (1980) indicate that individual tests are more effective than group ones. Sipay comments, "It is difficult, if not impossible, to measure word analysis skills accurately on a group test." (p. 5)

The main problem with individual tests is that they may take so much time that they are impractical for the classroom teacher to administer. Although not as valid as individual tests, a carefully constructed group test may still be useful.

Botel Reading Inventory. Modern Curriculum Press.

Accompanying the well-known *Botel Reading Inventory* is a nine-part decoding test. Included are subtests on letter recognition, words in simple phonograms or rhyming patterns, and words whose phonic patterns grow increasingly more difficult. These patterns range from CVC with short vowel words and common long vowel patterns to relatively difficult multisyllabic words. The final subtest contains multisyllabic pseudowords. The first three subtests, which evaluate letter recognition, matching of beginning consonants with sounds, and matching written pattern words to rhyming auditory patterns, can be administered to groups. The remaining six subtests must be given individually.

Diagnostic Analysis of Reading Errors. Jastak.

The examiner dictates forty-six words from the spelling section of the *Wide Range Achievement.* Students select the correct spelling from four printed choices. One option is a reversal, a second omits a sound, and a third contains a substitution. The fourth is the correct response. Responses are analyzed to see if there is a particular pattern of errors. The test is designed for secondary pupils.

Diagnostic Word Patterns, Tests 1, 2, 3. Educators Publishing Service.

Includes tests on three levels that can be used to diagnose spelling or phonics difficulties. Test 1 includes short vowel words accompanied by single consonants, various consonant clusters, and **ed.** Also tested are ten common sight words. Test 2 is composed of long vowel words, some **r** vowels, and a number of vowels that are neither long nor short nor r-controlled. Included, too, are ten sight words. Test 3 contains vowel combinations, suffixes, words that double the final consonant, multisyllabic words, and sight words.

Each test is composed of 100 words that may be dictated to the student or read by the student. The skill being tested is clearly marked and each skill is evaluated with ten items.

Doren Diagnostic Reading Test of Word Recognition Skills. American Guidance Service.

Areas tested include letter recognition, sight words, initial and final consonants, rhyming, vowel knowledge, blending and spelling.

GENERAL STANDARDIZED READING TESTS

Although they concentrate on comprehension and vocabulary, the major standardized group reading tests also assess phonics and other related word attack skills. Listed below are group reading tests and the skills that they cover.

California Achievement Tests. CTB/McGraw-Hill.

The *CAT* is published on eleven levels ranging from kindergarten to grade 12. Word attack skills are tested on the first eight levels. Initial and final consonants are assessed in Level 11. Initial and final clusters and digraphs are tested in Levels 11 to 13. Initial and final consonant digraphs are tested in Levels 14 to 16. Variant consonants are covered in Levels 15 and 16. Long vowels are included in Levels 11-13. Short vowels are tested in Levels 11-14. Other vowels are covered in Levels 12-16. Sight words and compound words are tested in Levels 11 and 12. Roots and affixes are assessed in Levels 11-16.

Comprehensive Test of Basic Skills. CTBS/McGraw-Hill.

The *CTBS* is published on nine levels ranging from kindergarten to high school. Word attack skills are assessed on the first four levels. Initial and final consonants are assessed in Levels B and C. Initial and final consonant clusters and digraphs and sight words are covered in Levels B-D. Short and long vowels are tested in Levels C-E. Other vowels are tested in Levels D and E. Identification of affixes, roots, components of a compound, and number of syllables in a word are assessed in Levels D and E. Contractions are covered in Level E.

Metropolitan Achievement Tests, MAT 6, Reading Diagnostic Tests. Psychological Corporation.

The *MAT Diagnostic Tests* come in six levels which range from kindergarten to ninth grade. Sight vocabulary is assessed on the first three levels. Knowledge of consonants is evaluated on the first five levels. Vowels and word parts are tested on the middle four levels. Word parts include compounds, affixes, and combining forms.

Stanford Achievement Tests. Psychological Corporation.

The Stanford is published on ten levels ranging from kindergarten through high school. The first six levels assess word attack skills.

Stanford Diagnostic Reading Test (3rd Ed.). Psychological Corporation.

The test comes in four levels: Red, Green, Brown, and Blue. The Red Level (grades 1.5-3.5) assesses auditory discrimination, beginning and ending consonants, consonant clusters and digraphs, and short and long vowels. The Green Level (3.0-5.5) tests auditory discrimination, multiple spellings of consonant sounds, and multiple spellings of long, short, and other vowels. Syllable division and correct blending of word and word parts into compound words and words with affixes are also tested. The Brown Level (5.0-9.5) assesses the ability to match multiple spellings of consonant and vowel sounds. (Students who can read on a fifth-grade level would not need to be tested on these skills since being able to read on a fifth-grade level is evidence that the pupil possesses basic phonic skills.) The Blue Level (8.5-13) assesses knowledge of affixes, combining forms, and roots in the context of real words. A test on structural analysis evaluates the ability to identify the correct syllabication of words. There is also a test on phonics, which is superfluous at this high level of reading achievement.

WORD ATTACK INVENTORY

The *Word Attack Inventory* was especially prepared for readers of this text. It was designed to provide an overview of students' decoding ability in several areas. Information from this informal measure should be supplemented by observation of students' actual performance as they apply word attack skills in a variety of reading situations.

Letter Recognition

Have students identify each of the following letters.
Upper Case

T S A E N C X H O G Q B Z M R J U P F V D Y I K L W

Lower Case

c y h m u r b e o i x s a t f n k l q z g p w j v d

Beginning Sounds

Before administering this subtest, make sure the student knows what is meant by beginning sounds. Tell the student that you are going to say two words. Ask him to listen to see if he can tell what is the same about the words. Say **key** and **king.** Discuss the fact that they begin with the same sound. Follow a similar procedure with **lock** and **ladder.**

Once students know what is meant by beginning sounds, tell them to: "Listen to these words. Which one begins with the same sound as **soap**?" Say: "**socks — cat — dog.** Which one begins like **soap**?" Give help as needed. Before administering the test, do the sample listed below.

The words in the first column are the test words.

Sample	man	bell	toy	map
1.	pot	moon	pie	sign
2.	dog	door	rake	wagon
3.	tie	map	name	tire
4.	ring	penny	deer	rug
5.	nail	saw	lamp	nest
6.	ball	nose	book	hand
7.	cake	cow	mouse	dish
8.	girl	jet	farm	game
9.	hat	sun	horse	key
10.	fish	foot	car	nail

Interpretation: An adequate performance would be 8/10 correct. A score below that suggests the need to work on perception of beginning sounds.

Beginning Consonants Correspondences

Tell the student being tested that you are going to ask him to read some words. Point out the words in Column A. Tell the student that each word ends with the sound /ā/. Ask the student to look at the first letter, think of the sound it stands for, and say the whole word. Do the first item as an example. Follow the same procedure with column B, /āk/, and Column C, /et/.

A	B	C
bay	bake	bet
day	fake	get
hay	lake	net
Jay	rake	vet
Kay	take	yet
may		
pay		
say		
way		

Interpretation: Getting 16 out of 20 suggests a fairly good grasp of initial consonants. Ultimately, students should know all the initial consonants. Work on weak items.

Ending Consonant Correspondences

For Column A, tell student that each word begins with /buh/. Ask the student to look at the last letter, think of the sound it stands for, and say each word. Do the first item as an example. Follow the same procedure with Column B, /hih/, and Column C, /tah/.

A	B	C
bub	hid	tab
bud	hill	tag
bug	him	tan
bum	his	tap
buff	hit	
bun		
bus		
but		

Interpretation: An adequate performance would be getting 14/17 correct. However, 100 percent is desirable. Work on weak items.

Consonant Clusters and Consonant Digraphs

For column A, tell the student that each word ends with /ā/. Ask the student to look at the letters and think of the sound or sounds they stand for, and say each word. Do the first item as an example. Follow the same procedure for Column B, /ān/ and Column C /āk/.

A	B	C
clay	brain	flake
gray	chain	snake
play	drain	shake
pray	grain	quake
tray	sprain	
slay	train	
spray		
stay		
stray		
sway		

Interpretation: An adequate performance is 16/20. However, a perfect performance is desirable. Work on weak items.

Short Vowels

Have the student read each of the following words. The information in parentheses indicates the skill being tested.

hat (**a** = /a/)	gym (**y** = /i/)
tell (**e** = /e/)	watch (**a** = /o/)
win (**i** = /i/)	son (**o** = /u/)
dot (**o** = /o/)	deaf (**ea** = /e/)

Interpretation: An adequate performance is 7/9. Note errors and work on weak items.

Long Vowels

Have the student read each of the following words. The information in parentheses indicates the skill being tested.

lake (**a-e** = /ā/)	told (**o** = /ō/)	nail (**ai** = /ā/)	way (**ay** = /ā/)
she (**e** = /ē/)	high (**igh** = /ī/)	leaf (**ea** = /ē/)	tile (**i-e** = /ī/)
rode (**o-e** = /ō/)	wheel (**ee** = /ē/)	buy (**y** = /ī/)	
so (**o** = /ō/)	row (**ow** = /ō/)	tie (**ie** = /ī/)	
cube (**u-e** = /ū/)	loaf (**oa** = /ō/)	chief (**ie** = /ē/)	

Interpretation: An adequate performance is 14/17. Note errors and work on weak items.

Other Vowels

Have student read each of the following words. The information in parentheses indicates the skill being tested.

hawk (**aw** = /aw/)	truth (**u** = /o͞o/)	choose (**oo** = /o͞o/)
coin (**oi** = /oi/)	prove (**o-e** = /o͞o/)	group (**ou** = /o͞o/)
tall (**al** = /aw/)	now (**ow** = /ow/)	fault (**au** = /aw/)
joy (**oy** = /oi/)	cost (**o** = /aw/)	stood (**oo** = /o͝o/)
threw (**ew** = /o͞o/)	shout (**ou** = /ow/)	due (**ue** = /o͞o/)

Interpretation: An adequate performance is 11/14. Note errors and work on weak items.

R Vowels

Have the student read each of the following words. The information in parentheses indicates the skill being tested.

share (**are** = /air/)	search (**ear** = /ər/)
year (**ear** = /ear/)	herd (**er** = /ər/)
firm (**ir** = /ər/)	wear (**ear** = /air/)
stair (**air** = /air/)	torn (**or** = /or/)
court (**our** = /or/)	curl (**ur** = /ər/)

Interpretation: An adequate performance is 8/10. Note errors and work on weak items.

Multisyllabic Words

The following multisyllabic words have been arranged in approximate order of difficulty. Have students read as many as they can. Stop after three errors in a row.

backyard	pumpkin	department
growling	decide	opportunity
friendly	robot	passage
unhappy	music	auditorium
careless	company	audience
alone	temperature	decoration
chapter	radiator	disappointment
shelter	emergency	apologize
postage	hesitation	congratulations
hotel	wonderful	automatically

Interpretation: Write down wrong responses and analyze errors. Look for patterns of strength and weakness.

Prefixes

The following words containing prefixes have been arranged in approximate order of difficulty. Have students read and explain the meaning of each word and point out the word's prefix. Stop after three errors in a row.

Basic	Advanced
unhappy	transAtlantic
replay	semicircle
incomplete	illegal
dishonest	propeace
preheat	ex-governor
impolite	coauthor
mispronounced	subgroup
nonfiction	antiwar
postgame	unicycle
superstar	irregular

Interpretation: Write down erroneous responses. Note level of performance and prefixes that posed problems.

Suffixes

The following words containing suffixes have been arranged in approximate order of difficulty. Have students read and explain the meaning of each word and point out the word's suffix. Stop after three errors in a row.

Basic	Advanced
quickly	historic
helpful	actual
homeless	leakage
worker	curiosity
wooden	assistant
believable	admittance
agreement	presidential
darkness	possession
adventurous	descriptive
cloudy	apologize

Interpretation: Write down erroneous responses. Note level of performance and suffixes that posed problems.

Combining Forms

The following words contain combining forms that have been arranged in approximate order of difficulty. Have students read each word and locate and explain the meaning of the combining form. The combining form is bold for your convenience. However, it should not be bold on the student's copy since part of the skill of understanding a combining form involves recognizing the combining form in the context of a word. Stop after three errors in a row.

1. **tri**motor
2. **mono**rail
3. speedo**meter**
4. **multi**colored
5. **kilo**gram
6. **aud**ible
7. oceano**grapher**
8. **deci**liter
9. **octo**syllable
10. **mega**dollars
11. **quad**ruplets
12. **deca**de
13. **milli**second
14. **poly**tonal
15. **geo**magnetic
16. **micro**second
17. **bio**physics
18. saxo**phone**
19. **auto**suggestion
20. **omni**present

Interpretation: Note level of student's performance and specific items that posed problems.

Dictionary Skills

Have students look up ten words that they found difficult in their reading. Students should be able to obtain an accurate pronunciation and appropriate definition for each word.

Interpretation: Note any difficulties that students have or slowness in performance. For instance, students might take an excessive amount of time to find the words or may have difficulty selecting appropriate definitions.

ADDRESSES OF PUBLISHERS

ADDISON-WESLEY PUBLISHING COMPANY
   One Jacob Way
   Reading, MA 01867
ALLIED EDUCATIONAL COUNCIL
   P.O. Box 78
   Galien, MI 49112
AMERICAN GUIDANCE SERVICE, INC.
   Publishers' Building
   Circle Pines, MN 55014
BARNELL LOFT, LIMITED
   958 Church Street
   Baldwin, NY 11510
BERTA-MAX, INC.
   P.O. Box 31849
   Seattle, WA 98103
THE CHILD'S WORLD
   980 N. McLean Boulevard
   Elgin, IL 60123
CHILDREN'S PRESS
   5440 N. Cumberland Avenue
   Chicago, IL 60656
CONTINENTAL PRESS
   520 East Bainbridge Street
   Elizabethtown, PA 17022
CTB/MCGRAW-HILL
   2500 Garden Road
   Monterey, CA 93940
CURRICULUM ASSOCIATES
   5 Esquire Road
   North Billerica, MA 01862-2589

DLM TEACHING RESOURCES
One DLM Park
P.O. Box 4000
Allen, TX 75002

E.P. DUTTON
2 Park Avenue
New York, NY 10016

EDUCATIONAL ACTIVITIES, INC.
1937 Grand Avenue
Baldwin, NY 11510

EDUCATIONAL TECHNOLOGY
P.O. Box 2377
Springfield, IL 62702

EDUCATORS PUBLISHING SERVICE, INC.
75 Moulton Street
Cambridge, MA 02238-9101

EMC PUBLISHING
300 York Avenue
St. Paul, MN 55101

ESSAY PRESS
P.O. Box 2323
La Jolla, CA 92037

ESSENTIAL LEARNING PRODUCTS COMPANY
P.O. Box 2607
Columbus, OH 43216

FOLLETT PUBLISHING COMPANY
1010 W. Washington Boulevard
Chicago, IL 60607

GARRARD PUBLISHING COMPANY
1607 N. Market Street
Champaign, IL 61820

GINN
Silver Burdett & Ginn
Simon & Shuster
160 Gould Street
Needham, MA 02194-2310

GOOD APPLE
Box 299
Carthage, IL 62321

GREEN WILLOW BOOKS
105 Madison Avenue
New York, NY 10016

HARCOURT BRACE JOVANOVICH
School Division
6277 Sea Harbor Drive
Orlando, FL 32887

HARPER & ROW
10 East 53rd St.
New York, NY 10022

HARTLEY COURSEWARE, INC.
2023 Aspen Glade
Kingwood, TX 77339

HAYES SCHOOL PUBLISHING COMPANY
321 Pennwood Avenue
Wilkensburg, PA 15221

HOUGHTON MIFFLIN COMPANY
Educational Software Division
Box 683
Hanover, NH 03755

INSTRUCTIONAL/COMMUNICATIONS TECHNOLOGY, INC.
10 Stepar Place
Huntington Station, NY 11746

JAMESTOWN PUBLISHERS
P.O. Box 99168
Providence, RI 02940

JASTAK ASSOCIATES, INC.
1526 Gilpin Avenue
Wilmington, DE 19806

KENDALL/HUNT PUBLISHING COMPANY
2460 Kerper Boulevard
Dubuque, IA 52001

LEAD EDUCATIONAL RESOURCES, INC.
32 Colony Road
Lexington, MA 02173

THE LEARNING COMPANY
P.O. Box 2168
Menlo Park, CA 94026-2168

LEARNING WELL
200 S. Service Road
Roslyn Heights, NY 11577

MCCARTHY-MCCORMACK, INC.
1440 Oak Hill Dr.
Colorado Springs, CO 80919

MCGRAW-HILL BOOK COMPANY
1221 Avenue of the Americas
New York, NY 10020

MCGRAW-HILL SCHOOL DIVISION
P.O. Box 25308
Oklahoma City, OK 73125

MECC
3490 Lexington Avenue
St. Paul, MN 55126

MEDIA MATERIALS
2936 Remington Avenue
Baltimore, MD 21211

CHARLES E. MERRILL PUBLISHING COMPANY
1300 Alum Creek Drive
Box 508
Columbus, OH 43216

MILLIKEN PUBLISHING COMPANY
1100 Research Boulevard
P.O. Box 21579
St. Louis, MO 63132

MODERN CURRICULUM PRESS
13900 Prospect Road
Cleveland, OH 44136

NEW READERS PRESS
1320 Jamesville Avenue, Box 131
Syracuse, NY 13210

PHONOVISUAL PRODUCTS, INC.
12216 Parkview Drive
P.O. Box 2007
Rockville, MD 20852

PROGRAM DESIGN INTERNATIONAL
798 North Avenue
Bridgeport, CT 06606

THE PSYCHOLOGICAL CORPORATION
555 Academic Court
San Antonio, TX 78204

QUEUE
562 Boston Avenue
Bridgeport, CT 06610

RANDOM HOUSE
201 East 50th Street
New York, NY 10022

THE RIVERSIDE PUBLISHING COMPANY
8420 Bryn Mawr Avenue
Chicago, IL 60631

FRANK SCHAFER PUBLICATIONS, INC.
19771 Magellen Drive
Torrance, CA 90502

SCHOLASTIC, INC.
P.O. Box 7501
2931 E. McCarty St.
Jefferson City, MO 65102

SCIENCE RESEARCH ASSOCIATES, INC.
155 N. Wacher Drive
Chicago, IL 60606

SCHOOLHOUSE PRESS, INC.
4700 Rockside Road
Independence, OH 44131

SOCIETY FOR VISUAL EDUCATION, INC.
1345 Diversey Parkway
Chicago, IL 60614

THE SMART ALEX PRESS
P.O. Box 7192
Quincy, MA 02169

STECK-VAUGHN COMPANY
P.O. Box 2028
Austin, TX 78768

TEACHER'S COLLEGE PRESS
    1234 Amsterdam Ave.
    New York, NY 10027

TEACHER SUPPORT SOFTWARE, INC.
    P.O. Box 7130
    Gainesville, FL 32605

WALKER AND COMPANY
    720 Fifth Avenue
    New York, NY 10019

WEEKLY READER/FIELD PUBLICATIONS
    245 Long Hill Road
    Middletown, CT 06457

WESTERN PUBLISHING COMPANY
    850 Third Avenue
    New York, NY 10022

YORK PRESS, INC.
    Box 369
    Monkton, MD 21111

ZANER-BLOSER
    2300 W. 5th Avenue
    P.O. Box 16764
    Columbus, OH 43216

REFERENCES

Anderson, R.C., Hiebert, E.H., Scott, J.A., & Wilkinson, I.A.G. (1985). *Becoming a nation of readers: The report of the Commission on Reading.* Washington: National Institute of Reading.

Aukerman, R. (1984). *Approaches to beginning reading* (2nd ed.). New York: Wiley.

Barrera, R. & Crawford, A.N. (1987). *Houghton Mifflin transition.* Boston: Houghton Mifflin.

Berliner, D.C. (1981). Academic learning time and reading achievement. In J.T. Guthrie (Ed.), *Comprehension and teaching: Research reviews.* Newark, DE: International Reading Association, 203-226.

Bloomfield, L. (1942). Linguistics and reading. *Elementary English Review, 19,* 125-130, 183-6.

Burling, R. (1970). *Man's many voices: Language in its cultural context.* New York: Holt, Rinehart, & Winston.

Carroll, J.B., Davis, P.C., & Richman, B. (1971). *The American Heritage word frequency book.* Boston: Houghton Mifflin.

Carus, M. (Ed.). (1985). *Headway.* Peru, IL: Open Court Publishing Company.

Chall, J.S. (1967). *Learning to read: The great debate.* New York: McGraw-Hill.

Chall, J.S. (1983). *Learning to read: The great debate* (Rev. ed.). New York: McGraw-Hill.

Cunningham, P.M. (1978). Decoding polysyllabic words: An alternative strategy. *Journal of Reading, 21,* 608-614.

Dale, E. & O'Rourke, J. (1971). *Techniques of teaching vocabulary.* Palo Alto, CA: Field.

Dale, E. & O'Rourke, J. (1976). *The living word vocabulary.* Chicago: World Book, Childcraft International.

Deighton, L.C. (1959). *Vocabulary development in the classroom.* New York: Columbia University Press.

Durkin, D. (1981). *Strategies for identifying words* (2nd ed.). Boston: Allyn & Bacon.

Dykstra, R. (1974). Phonics and beginning reading instruction. In C. Walcutt and others, *Teaching reading: A phonic/linguistic approach to developmental reading.* New York: Macmillan.

Ekwall, E.D. & Shanker, J.L. (1988). *Diagnosis and remediation of the disabled reader.* (2nd ed.). Boston: Allyn & Bacon.

Elkonin, D.B. (1973). Reading in the USSR. In J. Downing (Ed.), *Comparative reading.* New York: Macmillan, 551-579.

Farr R. & Carey, R.F. (1986). *Reading: What can be measured?* Newark, DE: International Reading Association.

Fernald, G.M. (1943). *Remedial techniques in basic school subjects.* New York: McGraw-Hill.

Fernald, G.M. & Keller, H. (1921). The effect of kinesthetic factors in the development of word recognition skills in the case of nonreaders. *Journal of Educational Research, 4,* 357-377.

Francis, W.N. (1983). *Dialectology: An introduction.* New York: Longman.

Gambrell, L.B., Wilson, R.N., & Gantt, W.N. (1981). Classroom observations of task-attending behaviors of good and poor readers. *Journal of Educational Research, 24,* 400-404.

Gillingham, A. & Stillman, B.W. (1960). *Remedial training for children with specific difficulty in reading, spelling, and penmanship* (7th ed.). Cambridge, MA: Educators Publishing Service.

Glass, G.G. & Burton, E.H. (1973). How do they decide? Verbalizations and observed behaviors of successful decoders. *Education, 94,* 58-65.

Glass, G.G. (1976). *Glass-analysis for decoding only. Teacher's guide.* Garden City, NY: Easier to Learn.

Goodman, K.S. & Goodman, Y.M. (1978). Reading of American children whose language is a stable rural dialect of English or a language other than English. Detroit, MI: Wayne State University. (Eric Document Reproduction Services. No. ED 173 754)

Gunning, T. (1975). *A comparison of word attack skills derived from a phonological analysis of frequently used words drawn from a juvenile corpus and an adult corpus.* Unpublished doctoral dissertation. Philadelphia, PA: Temple University.

Gunning, T. (1988). *Decoding behavior of good and poor second grade students.* Paper presented at the annual meeting of the International Reading Association, Toronto.

Guthrie, J.T. & Seifert, M. (1977). Letter-sound complexity in learning to identify words. *Journal of Educational Psychology, 69,* 686-696.

Harris, A.J. & Jacobson, M.D. (1982). *Basic reading vocabularies.* New York: Macmillan.

Harris, A.J. & Sipay, E.R. (1985). *How to increase reading ability* (8th ed.). White Plains, NY: Longman.

Hillerich, R. & Johnson, T. (1986). *Ready steps.* Boston: Houghton Mifflin.

Hardy, M., Stennett, R. & Smythe, P. (1973). Word attack: How do they "figure them out"? *Elementary English, 51,* 525-32.

Johnson, M.S. (1981). Research and the reality of reading. In C.M. Santa & B.L. Hayes (Eds.), *Children's prose comprehension, research and practice.* Newark, DE: International Reading Association, 133-156.

Johnson, M.S. & Kress, R.A. (1966). *Eliminating learning problems in reading disability cases.* Philadelphia, PA: Mimeographed.

Johnson, M.S., Kress, R.A., & Pikulski, J.J. (1987). *Informal reading inventories* (2nd ed.). Newark, DE: International Reading Association.

Kučera, H. & Francis, W.N. *Computational analysis of present-day American English.* Providence, RI: Brown University Press, 1967.

Labov, W. (1981). *The study of nonstandard English.* In V.P. Clark, P.A. Eschholz, & A.F. Rosa (Eds.), *Language: Introductory readings* (3rd ed.). New York: St. Martin's Press, 512-520.

Levin, H.M. (1985). *The educationally disadvantaged: A national crisis.* Philadelphia: Public/Private Ventures.

McKeown, M.G. (1985). The acquisition of word meaning from context by children of high and low ability. *Reading Research Quarterly, 20,* 482-496.

Marchbanks, G. & Levin, H. (1965). Cues by which children recognize words. *Journal of Educational Psychology, 56,* 57-61.

Matteoni, L., Sucher, F., Klein, M., & Welch, K. (1986). *Economy reading series.* Oklahoma City, OK.

Melmed, P.J. (1973). Black English phonology: The question of reading interference. In J.L. Laffey & R. Shuy (Eds.). *Language differences: Do they interfere?* Newark, DE: International Reading Association, 70-85.

Mish, F. (Ed.). (1983). *Webster's ninth new collegiate dictionary.* Springfield, MA: Merriam-Webster.

Nash, R. (1977). *Comparing English and Spanish: Patterns in phonology and orthography.* New York: Regents.

Neuman, S.B. (1981). A comparison of two methods of teaching vowel knowledge. *Reading Improvement, 18,* 264-269.

O'Brien, C.A. (1973). *Teaching the language-different child to read.* Columbus, OH: Merrill.

Pikulski, J.J. & Shanahan, T. (1980). A comparison of various approaches to evaluating phonics. *The Reading Teacher, 33,* 692-702.

Reed, C.E. (1977). *Dialects of American English* (Rev. ed.). Boston: University of Massachusetts Press.

Rubeck, P. (1977). Decoding procedures: Pupil self-analysis and observed behaviors. *Reading Improvement, 14,* 187-192.

Rosner, J. (1974). *Helping children overcome learning difficulties.* New York: Walker.

Samuels, S.J. (1967). Attentional processes in reading: The effect of pictures in the acquisition of reading responses. *Journal of Educational Psychology, 58,* 337-342.

Sartain, H.W. (1981). *Easiest sight words among high frequency words in a comprehensive reading vocabulary.* Paper given at annual meeting of International Reading Association, New Orleans.

Schatz, E.K. & Baldwin, R.S. (1986). Context clues are unreliable predictors of word meanings. *Reading Research Quarterly, 21,* 439-453.

Shuy, R.C. (1973). Nonstandard dialect problems: An overview. In J.L. Laffey & R.G. Shuy (Eds.), *Language differences: Do they interfere?* Newark, DE: International Reading Association.

Singer, H., Samuels, S.J., & Spiroff, J. (1973). The effect of pictures and contextual conditions on learning responses to printed words. *Reading Research Quarterly, 9,* 555-567.

Sipay, E.R. (1973). *Manual for the Sipay Word Analysis Tests.* Cambridge, MA: Educators Publishing Service.

Smith, N.B. (1965). American Reading Instruction (Rev. ed.). Newark, DE: International Reading Association.

Smitherman, G. (1981). "It bees dat way sometime": Sounds and structure of present-day Black English. In V.P. Clark, P.A. Eschholz, & A.F. Rosa (Eds.), *Language: Introductory readings* (3rd ed.). New York: St. Martin's Press, 521-538.

U.S. Department of Education (1986). *What works*. Washington, DC: U.S. Department of Education.

Wilson, R.C. & Rudolph, M.K. (1980). *Merrill Linguistic Reading Program* (3rd ed.). Columbus, OH: Merrill.

INDEX